FEMALE ENTREPRENEUR'S PLAYBOOK

SECRET STRATEGIES FROM 20+ WOMEN FOR BUILDING A BUSINESS YOU LOVE AND GETTING PAID FOR IT

FEMALE ENTREPRENEUR'S PLAYBOOK

LINDSEY ARDMORE & PATRICIA WOOSTER

Female Entrepreneur's Playbook: Secret Strategies From 20+ Women for Building a Business You Love and Getting Paid for It

First edition, October 2021

ISBN: 978-1-7368587-3-8

WosterMedia LLC
Tampa, Florida
woostermediabooks.com

Editing: Shayla Raquel, shaylaraquel.com

Published by WoosterMedia LLC
woostermediabooks.com

WoosterMedia

CONTENTS

FOREWORD

Many years ago, in the early days of Keap, I read a book called *Banker to the Poor* by Muhammad Yunus, the pioneer of micro-credit lending. In it, Yunis shared something that struck me like a lightning bolt. Yunus highlighted an insight he and his organization, Grameen Bank, had discovered as they loaned money to small business owners: *their female entrepreneur clients were much more successful than their male counterparts.*

Yunus went on to explain that female business owners had a higher success rate with Grameen's micro loan program. They had a much lower loan default rate. They were easier for the bank to work with. And they were more willing to apply the lessons learned from other Grameen clients. Grameen adapted its practices to loan money almost exclusively to female entrepreneurs. In the process, and contrary to social norms and popular opinion, Grameen built a successful micro-credit lending program. As a result, Grameen Bank has helped thousands of families and villages escape poverty as they and others like them change the world through micro lending.

The lesson from Yunus stood out to me because we noticed something similar in the early days of our company, as we provided entrepreneurs with our sales and marketing automation (SMA) platform. *We noticed that female entrepreneurs were more willing to do the hard setup work of SMA than were their male counterparts.* We saw success story after success story of women customers who burned the midnight oil to set up automation at night, while running their businesses during the day. We got to the point where my cofounder and I were almost surprised when a success story was *not* written by a female entrepreneur.

Since those early years, we have dramatically simplified the setup process of Keap's SMA software. Thankfully, we have countless success stories today from female and male entrepreneurs. But those early years at Keap taught me something I cannot deny:

> Female entrepreneurs tend to have a special drive that propels them through the difficult early challenges of entrepreneurship, helping them create a successful business and a better life for themselves and their families.

That's why I was so excited to learn about the *Female Entrepreneur's Playbook*. The more successful female entrepreneurs we see in the world, the greater the impact on families, communities, and economies.

Our purpose at Keap is to "liberate and empower entrepreneurs to strengthen families, communities, and economies." We know that automation is the great game changer for entrepreneurs. We see women entrepreneurs having a massive impact on the world and we are excited to champion their efforts in every way possible. We are especially passionate about female entrepreneurs because the family is often central to their business pursuits. One of the underlying tenets of our business is that families are strengthened when entrepreneurs successfully automate their sales and marketing.

Now, having said that, the practical realities of entrepreneurship can become all-consuming. When entrepreneurs start a business, they have dreams of freedom, impact, and money that will bless them and their families. But all too often, the business demands more than the entrepreneur can deliver and the dreams of freedom, impact, and money go down the drain. The cost of failed entrepreneurship is very high, often tallied in more significant measures than dollars. When an entrepreneur fails in their business, all too often it costs the entrepreneur relationships, health, creativity, and even the very identity of the entrepreneur. At Keap, we call this "the dark side of entrepreneurship."

As a community of entrepreneurs, we can do better for our fellow entrepreneurs.

That's why this book is so important. This book shows the way to female entrepreneurs, sparing them from mistakes made by other successful entrepreneurs. We all have to learn by making mistakes. But if we can accelerate our progress by learning from *others'* mistakes, we are much more successful and that path to success is much less painful.

Over the years, I've watched many female entrepreneurs juggle the demands of business, family, and personal life. There's an art to it that I cannot fully appreciate as a male entrepreneur. I saw my mom do it. I've watched my sisters do it. I've been impressed by the many women in my life who love business and family and strive to excel in both. While I certainly know how difficult it is to balance life as an entrepreneur, I'm especially intrigued and in awe of the female entrepreneurs who do this well. It's worth it for *all* entrepreneurs to pay attention and learn how successful female entrepreneurs balance business, family, and life.

Finally, I'm excited about this book because I personally know many of the successful female entrepreneurs highlighted here. You see, the common thread among successful customers we saw all those years ago at Keap continues to run through the company today. Many of our top partners and customers are successful female entrepreneurs, several of whom are highlighted in this book. These women want to empower female entrepreneurs, and they do it every day in their businesses. It's a thrill for me to see them using Keap in their work and contributing to "The Keap Family" of customers, partners, and employees working to empower entrepreneurs through sales and marketing automation.

The authors of this book have a passion for helping female entrepreneurs succeed. They freely share their hacks, successes, and failures. They genuinely care about your success, and they are eager to help you along your quest for freedom as an entrepreneur.

Whatever stage of entrepreneurship you're in, I applaud you for picking up this book. Now, sit back, take it all in, and enjoy putting their wisdom to work in your business.

Keep going, keep serving, keep growing!

Clate Mask

CEO and Cofounder of Keap

INTRODUCTION

Hi there. Welcome to the *Female Entrepreneur's Playbook*. We're so happy you're here. Since you've chosen to read this book, we assume you're on your own business journey, whether you are just starting out or well on your way. You may be changing careers, making a pivot, or ready to seriously level up your dreams. Wherever you are in the process, we are here to encourage you and be supportive allies.

But before you dive into the magic contained within these chapters, we want to make sure you understand how absolutely divine you are. It might sound strange at the beginning of a book, but we know that all of our authors agree that our gifts in business are divine as female entrepreneurs. We are blessed to create change from thin air. We can pull money out of the sky with every sale. We make the world a better place, lift our economies, and bring the most beautiful energy and soul to clients, families, and communities.

Please don't ever forget that. Because being an entrepreneur is messy, terrifying, exhilarating, rewarding, and amazing—sometimes all at once. It's a roller-coaster ride that ebbs and flows but allows us to make an impact even in the toughest of times.

Now, the contents of this book can be business-changing if applied. In each chapter, you'll hear from different successful female entrepreneurs who run diverse types of businesses. You will get to know them, and more importantly, you'll get to sit at the table with them. We created this book with the sincere intention that you (whether brand new or seasoned business pro) get a behind-the-scenes look at how successful women are building their empires.

You're going to learn what drove each woman to success and what inspires them now. They share how they make their money, their most worthwhile business investments, and what they would do differently if they were starting over.

From the very beginning of this project, we have told everyone that this book is the mastermind we always wish we had . . . the book we need sitting on our desks . . . the book that offers hope and provides answers. It is meant to be consumed, to be marked up, and to inspire you to take action.

We have personally gotten to know each woman, and to hear their stories is to love them. We have women who have survived insurmountable odds, dealt with heartbreak and sorrow, quit everything to back themselves, and suffered loss (of family, friends, and business). Women who refused to sacrifice their family time for their business, women who continued to show up when it was hard, defeating, and overwhelming. Women who are out there every day crushing it and creating the business and life of their dreams.

Our sincere wish is that you walk away feeling enlightened, empowered, and encouraged. Nothing would make us happier than to know that you were able to implement strategies, learn lessons, and quantum leap your business forward.

Finally, before you dive in, know that this book was designed for you. Every word, every sentence, every paragraph was designed and painstakingly crafted just for you. Make no mistake: These women are successful for a reason. So breathe in their words and find the pieces that speak to your soul.

As you embark on your own successful journey, we would like to share one final thought: Your success is not determined by the amount of money you make or the number of clients you serve. Success is determined by the amount of try in your heart. We hope you enjoy this book and have massive takeaways that impact your business and life. More importantly, we hope you connect with these authors. Find them on social media and share your thoughts. We would love nothing more.

To Your Incredible Success,
Lindsey Ardmore & Patricia Wooster

I WANT TO SHOW WOMEN A PEACEFUL WAY TO CONQUER THEIR FEARS AND DO SOMETHING THAT IS HARD, BUT THAT IS ALSO REWARDING BEYOND MEASURE.

Lindsey Ardmore

CHAPTER 1

AUTOMATION LEADS TO FREEDOM BY LINDSEY ARDMORE

The moment the doctor laid my new baby girl on my chest, I realized that I was never going back to work. The feeling of pure elation after a normal, but also terrifying, birth was squashed by the fear of leaving this little newborn with a sitter. I had been told many horror stories of abusive babysitters throughout my pregnancy, and they all came to a head at that moment.

The day I got home from the hospital, with a newborn snuggled close to my chest, I took stock of everything that I could do. Up until this point, I had worked for the previous three years as the chief operating officer of a business consulting company. I had skills, but nothing I felt was tangible. I didn't know it at the time, but imposter syndrome was a raging beast inside of me. I decided to list myself on a freelancing website doing tech support for small businesses for twenty-five dollars per hour.

From that moment on, my life has never been the same.

By the time my daughter (and brand-new business!) was a week old, I had replaced my corporate income. Within six months, I had made $200,000. But that quick success was quickly balanced by a lack of boundaries and long working hours. I spent hours per day in business after business helping automate tasks that would eventually put me out of a job. It didn't take long for me to start feeling the effects of postpartum depression and burnout. I wasn't showering, I wasn't sleeping, and I wasn't spending any time with the little girl who prompted this huge life shift.

It was around this same time that I retired my husband from his accounting position and we made a trip to California for a business conference. My life changed at that conference. My eyes were opened to a new way of thinking and doing business—a way that didn't require me to work twelve to fifteen hours a day, a way that encouraged having a life outside of work, a way that gave me forecastable income. I credit that trip for taking me from six figures in my first year to doubling, then tripling my income over the next few months and into the next few years.

At the conference, I realized that even though I was an automation expert (and a Keap Certified Partner) and had systems and processes for marketing and growing a business, I didn't actually implement any of that for myself. I was too busy battling imposter syndrome, dealing with postpartum depression, and white-knuckling my way through my life and business. My burnout was becoming obvious to everyone, and I knew I needed to do something different.

That's when I got really serious about my boundaries and realized that nobody would hold the boundary for me. It was like one day, I just decided not to let another day go by wishing something was different. I had to *be* different. And that shift, well, it honestly saved my life.

When I started enjoying my daughter, my husband, and my business again without all the constant anxiety and spiraling I was doing previously, I became more productive, more inspired, and healthier both mentally and physically.

I bought a horse, had a second child, and moved across single-minded planted roots in a place we now hope to live forever.

These shifts have enabled me to make multiple six figures of income and work six to eight hours per week, allowing me to focus on the things that really matter to me and my well-being.

But most importantly, the growth my business has seen is directly related to the hundreds of thousands of dollars that I've helped women around the world make in their businesses. In the past five years, Star Tower Systems and Team Lindsey have expanded to support female entrepreneurs not only to automate their businesses, but also to put their sales on autopilot so they can spend more time doing what they love . . . instead of what they have to do to make ends meet.

What is your *why* or purpose for your business?

If you had asked me this question five years ago as I snuggled with my newborn baby, I would have told you she was my only *why*. I didn't care about mission, values, or purpose at that point. I was single-minded about staying home.

But over my time in business, I've realized that I have a more divine errand here on this planet. And that is my true why and purpose for my business.

I am deeply passionate about women doing whatever the *heck* they want to do with their lives.

For some of us, that's building a business so we can stay home, be with our children, and show up as good wives and mothers.

For others, it's about creating a lifestyle that isn't tied to a desk, expectations, and the "traditional way" of doing things. And those are my ladies. The rule breakers, the renegades, and the powerhouses. Because, honestly, those women suffer more than *anyone* with imposter syndrome and their feelings of "not enoughness."

I want to show women a peaceful way to conquer their fears and do something that is hard, but that is also rewarding beyond measure. I want them to see the pitfalls and the mistakes that we've been conditioned and predisposed to make, because I know that they can overcome them.

I want them to *know*, in their hearts and deep into their souls, that they are valuable, that they are loved completely and unconditionally, and that they have divine gifts that need to be shared with the world.

When I look at the women in my life, whether they are friends, family, or clients, I see their unstoppable potential. And I want them to see that too.

I look at the woman who is struggling to get her business off the ground, struggling to make any real money, and sacrificing all of her time, talents, and energy to just "make it work," and I want to be there for her. I want her to have the tools in her tool kit to make her wildest dreams come true.

It's not going to be easy for her, but it will definitely be worth the work. And *that* is the message I feel called to share.

What are the biggest mistakes you see new entrepreneurs making?

There are three big mistakes that I watch entrepreneurs make every single day, whether they are new to business or seasoned. Those mistakes are hustling and grinding in the business but not making any real money; jumping around to random marketing strategies because of shiny-object syndrome; and working hard to get leads interested but doing little to follow up and then feeling guilty about it.

Each of those is totally crippling and so common, it's not even funny.

Mistake #1: Hustling and grinding in the business but not making any real money.

Unfortunately, this is *way* too common with the women (and cool dudes!) I work with. They work really, really hard, grinding themselves down into the ground, but they don't make any real money. At least not enough to make them feel like all of that hard work was worth it.

But why is that? Why do we take ourselves to burnout so consistently? Nobody wants to be burnt out!

It's because we've been told our entire lives that hard work equals success. To be successful, you had to get good grades. Or success looks like going to school for years and years and becoming a doctor or a lawyer, and anything short of that isn't "success." Our society also conditions us to believe that easy money, or money that doesn't come from the sweat of our back, is too good to be true or a Ponzi scheme. We shy away from making things easier on ourselves, and that's a true problem.

Because how can you add *more* to your plate if you're already maxed out on time and burning yourself out?

It's actually nonsensical!

So what is the antidote to this? The antidote is to automate, delegate, and delete. Stop focusing on all the things and focus on the things that generate revenue in your business. It's too easy to fall into the trap of wearing a busy badge and not getting paid a cent because you're focused on the wrong things.

That's why I love and teach automation: it takes you out of the weeds and focuses the business on revenue generation while you're doing the things you love and are best at.

Mistake #2: Jumping around to random marketing strategies because of shiny-object syndrome.

Don't laugh. This is probably you or someone you know! Shiny-object syndrome is a debilitating disease that disproportionately affects female entrepreneurs.

Maybe this looks like launching a lead magnet, then a small intro offer, a new lead magnet, starting a bot, or a podcast, and doing, doing, doing. But once again, there is no revenue being generated and a sad little entrepreneur working her tail off.

Why is that? Why do we do this? Because it's easier to jump around and believe that a strategy doesn't work instead of facing the reality that maybe it wasn't perfect and needs to be tweaked.

It's okay to try things and experiment. But it's critical that you take yourself out of the foundation of your business as quickly as possible so you can stop sabotaging your sales. I know. I'm triggering. It's fine.

I believe there are seven core foundational functions that every business needs to have, and without these seven functions, you don't have a business. You have a terrible source of overwhelm!

These core functions are what I call the Business Blueprint.

Before you start floating off to la-la land, please note that every successful business out there follows the Business Blueprint. Think of it as a universal law. It just is. Your business either has one or needs one.

The core functions of the Business Blueprint are:

1. Attracting traffic
2. Capturing leads
3. Nurturing relationships
4. Converting to cash
5. Delivering and wowing
6. Creating lifetime customers
7. Spreading the love

But when you're running through each function manually (which many coaches and consultants tend to do), you aren't spending time doing the things that fill your cup, light you up, make life easy, and give you the fulfillment that you're always looking for.

And when you're dealing with shiny-object syndrome, these seven core functions are often completely thrown to the side and cripple the business.

However, if these seven core functions are automated, your business can make sales "automagically" while you're focusing on your zone of genius or true talents.

Mistake #3: Working hard to get leads interested but doing little to follow up and then feeling guilty about it.

Have you ever busted your bum to get people interested in working with you, and then you never talk to them again?

Have you ever had a sales call where you forgot to send the lead a follow-up?

Have you ever gotten a business card (old school, I know!) and then promptly dropped it on your desk, never to look at it again ... even though the person said to give them a call to chat about what you do?

I could go on and share twenty more examples, but I'm sure you're already looking inward to how many people you need to send a follow-up to, right?

This lack of follow-up is crippling your business. *And you're the bottleneck*. It's not fun, but it's the truth. If you didn't drop everybody on their heads after a sales call or after interest was sparked, your business revenue would look a *lot* different.

So why do we do this? Why do we insist on working so hard and then just dropping everyone off on the corner without a way to get a hold of us? It's got a lot to do with imposter syndrome, overwhelm, and general lack of time and resources.

You're only human. And this is the exact reason I am so passionate about automation and taking you out of the equation.

Imagine if everyone you spoke to or took an interest in your services was nurtured and loved upon.

Imagine if you didn't have to scramble for sales every single month.

Imagine a business that didn't require you to be hustling and grinding every single day.

That kind of business is easy and, most importantly, peaceful when you automate your Business Blueprint. And it's 100 percent possible for you.

How have you diversified your revenue streams within your business?

Have you heard the saying that the average seven-figure business has seven streams of income? I'm not sure if that's true, but I'm a big believer that you don't have to make your money with one program, one offering, or one tool.

The reality is that some of our personalities and designs are just not meant to operate with one flow, and that's okay.

I've found that having low-ticket, mid-ticket, and high-ticket offerings that all work together has been the most successful in my business. My value ladder has been carefully culled over the years, and I have found that changing up my low-ticket offerings through paid workshops, memberships, and other low-cost products have helped maintain my "I make sales every day" goal. My mid-range product is in the form of a gorgeous program called Automation Foundations, which helps automate the Business Blueprint that I shared above. After launching that in 2018, I was dedicated to serving as many women as possible through that program. Watching women step out of their way, start making sales on autopilot, and growing their business while on vacation, spending time with kids, or doing what makes their hearts happy has truly been the honor of a lifetime.

I also think it's important to diversify through affiliate commissions and supporting other businesses. As a Keap Certified Partner, I make commissions off every sale, but it's an absolute no-brainer to keep sharing when you partner with brands and products you love. Many women shy away from creating and sharing affiliate partnerships, but the opportunities I've gotten from Keap are to the tune of over $200,000 in passive income. I encourage all female entrepreneurs to cultivate partnerships to grow their businesses in a very passive way.

What hard lessons have you learned that could have been avoided?

Quite a few!

1. Ask questions before signing contracts.
2. Always protect your energy; energy vampires are real and ready to suck the life out of you.
3. Look for the positives each day with gratitude and mindfulness.
4. Set boundaries and hold boundaries. Nobody else cares about your boundaries; you are responsible for making them work.
5. Don't hire expensive experts when you're not paying yourself.
6. Implement a budgeting/money system (I like Profit First) right away.
7. Make decisions to keep moving forward and know that they can be changed in an instant.
8. As an entrepreneur, you create money out of thin air. When you're not making sales, you're not in the act of creation.
9. Fire clients who make you feel nervous or anxious to speak to them; that's called a red flag.
10. Always be kind to your peers, your colleagues, your clients, and most importantly yourself.

What is your biggest day-to-day struggle in running your business?

Energy! People think I have a lot of energy and drive because I show up often in live videos, all over social media, and I'm constantly educating and inviting. However, that couldn't be further from the truth.

My energy comes in waves, like the ocean. Some days, I have boundless energy. Other days, I'm fighting to get anything done.

When I realized that my energy ebb and flow greatly benefited me, I began to protect it a lot more and stopped trying to hustle, grind, and force results.

I used to think I wasn't motivated enough or smart enough or talented enough, or that I was suffering from something more serious. After getting conscious about my health and personality, I realized that my energy is really sensitive. I need lots of downtime so that when I have high energy, I can explode like a supernova!

So while yes, it's a daily struggle, getting clarity on my energy has been hugely empowering. Sleeping in, taking naps, relaxing with my two children, and generally being mindful have changed how I show up as a wife, mother, and business owner.

If you lost everything today, what would you do for the next thirty days to generate income?

Anything and everything I needed to do! Also, why did I lose everything? Did my gambling finally get the best of me?

Just kidding. I don't gamble. But I do love a certain degree of risk. I guess that's why I'm an entrepreneur.

But in all seriousness, thirty days is plenty of time to generate income, and it doesn't have to be with paid advertising, selling your soul to the devil, or insane hours.

I would make sure I had a strategic plan in place on how much money I needed and the things I was willing to sell or do to get there. It's really simple: If you need $10,000 and your offering is $10,000, how are you going to get one person to purchase it?

Now, it's not that simple in reality, but having a plan in place is the best way to make sure you are in alignment and feel comfortable to work toward that goal. I always say that a strategy is just an intention. It's just meant to give you the end point so you're not feeling your way around in the dark.

Now, I'm not going to tell you to do one specific thing or show up in one specific way. I don't think that's helpful and might not align with how you choose to do business.

Instead, I would love for you to write down strategies or actions that you've done in the past that have been successful. Let's also use the term "successful" loosely, because I'm sure the first thought that popped into your brain was, "But I've never been successful!" Hello, imposter syndrome. Can you leave us alone now?

Write those strategies down, then write down what you want to sell. What offer would you love people to take advantage of? How have you sold it previously? Is that something that's repeatable this week? Next week? What are you waiting for? Get after it!

How can people connect with you?

I can be found at lindseyardmore.com and on Instagram @lindseyardmore.

I WORK WITH INSPIRING PEOPLE FROM ALL WALKS OF LIFE AND HELP THEM BRING THEIR GENIUS OUT INTO THE WORLD.

Patricia Wooster

CHAPTER 2

CREATE YOUR IMPACT BY PATRICIA WOOSTER

You can't make money as a writer. Those were the encouraging words I received two weeks before I graduated college with a degree in creative writing. It's amazing how fast a person can go from being idealistic and passionate about a career to looking for a safe job that pays the bills. But that's exactly what I did. I absorbed all of the expectations, fears, and conservative views of those around me. This is before the internet and online jobsites made it easy to apply for jobs worldwide. I only knew about available positions through *The Kansas City Star* newspaper, and "writing" was not a hirable category.

My first "real" job was in a huge call center where we sold computers in cow-spotted boxes. I spent the following ten years moving from one software sales position to the next until I finally landed in Tampa, Florida. I did not write during this time. Instead, I wined and dined with huge corporate clients like Disney, Publix, and Home Shopping Network. The money was great, my coworkers were fun, but I found no passion in my work. When I became pregnant at age thirty-one, I knew I would not return from maternity leave. The day before my son was born, I closed a deal that funded his college account. That was the last time I worked for someone else.

Being a full-time mom was fulfilling, but my son was a serious napper. All of my friends worked, and I was bored, so I decided to write a novel. It took months and months, and it was terrible. A friend who wrote work-for-hire books suggested I try fact-checking to earn extra money, learn the craft of writing books, and network with publishers. For those who don't know, nonfiction books go through a fact-checking process where all statements of fact need to be checked for accuracy and annotated. Even those little picture books go through this process.

Within two years, I fact-checked over three hundred books and accumulated a Rolodex full of publishing contacts. Here's an insider fact: the first drafts of most of these books are bad. As I developed better relationships with editors, I started leaving notes on the manuscripts with suggested changes to improve the books. To one major publisher, I said, "Even I can write a better book than this." Two weeks later, they gave me an opportunity to prove it and assigned me a book to write. This was the start of my writing career.

My entry point to major publishers like Simon & Schuster was through a side door where I built the relationship first. I didn't begin with a query letter, book proposal, or agent. I started with assigned projects and then verbally pitched my book ideas to an editor at Simon & Schuster. My friends in the author community laugh because I did everything wrong. I didn't follow protocol. I utilized the skills I learned in corporate sales to get to the gatekeeper. People forget there's more than one way to skin a cat. I've traditionally published thirteen nonfiction books. Some have sold well, and others have not. My books have been used in school curriculums, put me on stage, got me featured at WE Day, and even landed me two board of director positions. It's been quite the journey.

And just when I thought I was living my purpose, self-publishing became a major trend. Every businessperson started writing books. Vanity publishers popped up overnight and preyed upon first-time writers. I was invited to "pick your brain" coffee dates by professional women in my community. They were getting terrible advice about how to write and publish a book.

Over coffee, one of these women asked me to coach her through the process, so technically, she started my book-coaching business for me. Now I work with leaders, entrepreneurs, athletes, and all kinds of amazing people who want to create an impact with their words. Some choose to go the traditional publishing path, and others self-publish their books. Either way, we always adhere to the high standards set by the Big Five publishers (soon to be Big Four), which are the top publishing companies in the industry.

I love my job, and my clients inspire me. I don't always know what I'm doing, but I figure it out. When I started in this industry, I had zero connections, no experience, and a LinkedIn profile representing an entirely different career. My relationships, perseverance, and willingness to learn have gotten me here. It's why I can now confidently say, "You can *absolutely* make money as a writer."

What is your *why* or purpose for your business?

When I first became an entrepreneur, my *why* was to earn an income while staying home with my kids. Many of those side hustles were a way to stay busy and make a little extra money. I stopped and started a lot of different things. My real passion was writing, but I treated it like a hobby for many years.

My true purpose developed with the publication of my first book. It's an amazing experience to create something, put it out into the world, and discover that your words impact someone. I rinsed and repeated that process thirteen times before I started helping others. Book coaching allows me to merge my corporate experience with my passion for writing. It's the best of both worlds. I work with inspiring people from all walks of life and help them bring their genius out into the world.

Books, to me, are the ultimate legacy. People from all over the world can discover who you are just by finding your book on Amazon or in a bookstore. They are the best way to name and claim your methodologies, expertise, and create a transformation for someone. Once you write a book, you can create an entire ecosystem around it with things like public speaking, digital courses, workshops, live events, coaching, and consulting. And while all of those things help grow your business, they also make the information you are sharing super sticky. Imagine the positive impact you can have on others if they are able to learn and implement what you are teaching.

I have firsthand experience of the power just one book can have on a person's life. Several years ago, after a rather intense lung surgery, I was homebound for many months. Reading the book *The Miracle Morning* by Hal Elrod changed my life. Through his book and online program, I was able to build a morning routine that significantly improved my health and mental well-being. Ultimately, it changed my entire business too, because now I only work with people writing high-impact books.

Which activities do you perform that generate the majority of your revenue?

My primary offers are coaching, digital courses, ghostwriting, and book sales. Most of my revenue comes from high-ticket one-on-one book coaching with the average client contract lasting six months. I don't need a high volume of sales to hit my goals with this offer, but I am interested in diversifying into more passive income opportunities through my books and digital courses. Every week, I use a combination of the following activities to grow and scale my business:

- Referrals: I ask for referrals and testimonials from everyone I meet. It is key to utilize reviews and testimonials on your website, sales pages, and social media posts.
- Clubhouse: This audio-only social media platform has exponentially grown my business this year. By hosting regular weekly rooms, I've been able to build the like, know, and trust factors with thousands of new people. Many of these connections have followed me on Instagram, joined my email list, and purchased my digital offers.
- Partnerships: I've learned how to partner with people who are already talking to my ideal audience. The book you are reading now is the result of one of those partnerships. Collaborating with complementary businesses has allowed me to scale and create new offers.

What is one of your greatest failures that ultimately led to success?

A few years ago, I signed an amazing book contract with Simon & Schuster. Anyone who is in the book industry knows that getting an offer from one of the Big Five publishers is a pretty exciting deal. I felt like this was my make-or-break moment. As someone who loves to write, I was super intense during the writing of my first draft. I was so focused on the *writing* that I forgot to do one extremely important thing: marketing.

I didn't post on social media, build an email list, or even talk about my book outside of my family and circle of friends. I thought it was the responsibility of the marketing department of the publishing company to create interest and excitement for it. I was too naive about the industry to understand how rare it was for a virtual nobody with no online presence, audience, or name recognition to get a book deal. I expected print placements and media to magically appear because the early reviews from Publisher's Weekly and Kirkus Reviews were very good.

But I was *very* wrong and I discovered this quite abruptly. A few weeks before my book's release date, the person in charge of the marketing department quit her job. All of us debut authors were told to move forward with our marketing and launch strategies as planned. *What launch plan?* I thought. *I don't have a plan.*

That's when I found out that the author is responsible for the publicity and sales of their book. The publishing company is there to support the author but doesn't have the resources or capacity to do the implementation. With less than two weeks to my release date, I needed a plan, because everyone knows: If your book doesn't earn out its advance, then there are no more book deals.

I didn't have time to create a social media presence or anything else that required time and consistency. Instead, I looked for short-term opportunities to maximize sales, which led me to bulk sales. I created a list of schools, nonprofits, associations, and corporations aligned with my book's topic. Next, I developed curriculum, workshops, and speaking topics to bundle with it so I could pitch a complete solution.

I sold thousands of books with this strategy. I discovered that it's just as easy to sell many books to one person as it is to sell one-to-one. It allows your book to create a bigger impact because it's bundled with additional content and it's being utilized by a group of people together. It's become my absolute favorite way to launch and sell books. This sales tactic is transferable and works with selling digital courses, workbooks, consulting, and products.

Just as a side note, my failure to build a platform for my books or offers has only happened once. I understand the importance of playing the long game of building a network, online presence, and email audience. People love to have a behind-the-scenes look at how you are writing your book, creating your course, and developing your offerings. I've found this to be the easiest type of content to create and the most impactful for my followers. They can learn from the successes and failures, while still being a part of the journey. Once a product/service is ready for launch, they feel vested in and want to experience the result, which transfers to sales.

What hard lessons have you learned that could have been avoided?

I started out trying to do everything myself, thinking it would save me either time or money. It did neither. There are so many skills to learn as an entrepreneur, especially technical things like funnels, social media, websites, software, and design. Or when it comes to upleveling with hiring, accountability, pricing, and creating offers. There are so many new things to learn, and the list grows as you become more successful.

My advice is to invest in the best possible help you can afford. Don't try to do everything yourself. It isn't efficient or necessary. Utilize the expertise of those around you to get the best practices, advice, and shortcuts to getting the results you want. Coaching is a tax write-off and one of the most valuable investments you can make.

It was a conversation with a coach that changed my entire business and mindset. We met for my quarterly call, and I was so excited to share my progress. Every objective I had set was accomplished, but as she read through my report, she did not look happy. Instead of a congratulations, she asked, "How much money have you made so far this year?"

I prefaced my answer with, "This has been more of a creation year, so the numbers are a bit low."

Her response: "What was *so* important for you to create that you couldn't double your numbers from last year? Because from where I'm standing, you already have the expertise, credibility, and experience. What you don't have is sales or marketing."

Lack of marketing was surfacing again. I learned my lesson on launching, marketing, and promoting myself as an author, but I still struggled with seeing myself as a brand or business. I operated on referrals. I never pitched or sold anything, even though I had courses and coaching available.

It was so bad that when I sent a newsletter to my list about a new course offering, someone got upset. He couldn't believe I was trying to sell him anything. It was the first time I ever mentioned a product or service in a newsletter. This particular subscriber had received my emails for three years.

I was incorporated as a business but still operated as a freelancer. As I transitioned into courses, workshops, and working with coaches to bring books (like the one you are reading) to their mastermind members, I needed to build an audience of buyers. Working with coaches, mentors, and accountability partners has taught me to change my mindset around sales and marketing. Every person who works with me and writes a book creates an impact with their audience. This is a high-value service, so it's imperative I give people the opportunity to participate in my programs. Oftentimes, people are not purchasing because they do not know you or know your offers exist.

What have you found helps with blending your personal and professional life?

The first thing that I can say as someone who runs a business from their home is to have a plan. More importantly, this plan needs to work for you and your family. The way I structure my business and life breaks about every rule most business coaches advise, but it works for me.

I work seven days a week but have a ton of time where I do not work. I reserve two days a week for my one-on-one coaching clients and then focus on my other projects, administration, and marketing during the other days. During the week, I've found I work best in small increments with lots of breaks in between. Sometimes it's a long break so I can sit by the pool or hang out with my kids. Or a short break may involve a book or watching an episode of my favorite show.

On weekends, I piddle around with my personal writing projects or an online course I'm excited to take. I love what I do, so very little of it feels like work. My sons know they can come into my office at any time, and one of them edits all of my videos. It's a very casual environment when I'm not on coaching calls.

As an introvert, it's important to have the space to recharge. Some people take entire days off from work. I take days off from clients and speaking. This includes apps like Clubhouse, Facebook, and Instagram where I interact with other people. I use this white space to concentrate on writing my books, research, and creating digital offers. It gives me time to learn new skills and reenergize.

If you lost everything today, what would you do for the next thirty days to generate income?

If I lost my business, products, and programs, then I would immediately map out a plan of action. We all have expertise that is transferable and unique based on our experiences and education. I'd create a list of all those things and look for a way to combine some of them into a signature program. For example, I have traditional publishing experience, worked with Fortune 500 companies, and am good at creating messaging around people's zone of genius. My signature program could be "How to Outline and Write a High-Impact Book" and target executives. Based on this idea, I'd structure my next four weeks in the following ways:

- Step 1: Create a sales page for a $97 workshop based on my signature program. This is where I'd sell the *why* and *what* of my methodology. Also, I'd make sure that the deliverable for the workshop was very clear so they walk away with a very high-value result. At the end of the workshop, I'd offer a discounted coaching call to discuss what they came up with during the workshop and offer feedback. Hopefully, this converts to long-term coaching.

- Step 2: I'd take the recordings from this workshop and remove the interactive components with the participants and utilize the training portion to create a $47 low-ticket online course. I'd add an introduction, some done-for-you templates, and a workbook. I could do this in a day and have it available with a sales page within forty-eight hours.
- Step 3: Start writing a book on the same topic as the workshop and online course. Obviously, I can't finish it within thirty days, but that's not my objective during this thirty-day plan. My goal is to build an audience for my workshop and course. By documenting my writing process on social media—Instagram, in my case—I'm bringing people along on my journey. People love a behind-the-scenes look, and it gives me the opportunity to share my expertise without constantly selling.
- Step 4: Run my workshop every week. Based on conversion percentages from previous programs, this is my revenue projection for each workshop with fifteen attendees:
  - Workshop: $97 x 15 attendees = $1,455.
  - Four of them opt in for the discounted coaching call for $150 = $600.
  - One signs up for a $3,000 coaching package.
  - Workshop total: $5,055
- Step 5: Reinvest some of the first workshop's revenue into Facebook ads for the low-ticket online course. The purpose of selling the course is to convert cold leads into leads for the high-ticket coaching business. A combination of ads and followers on Instagram should create interest in me and my low-risk offer.
- Step 6: Keep writing my book. Publishing a book around my zone of genius or unique methodology allows me to put a stake in the ground by naming and claiming my expertise.

It's a foundational piece for me to create opportunities in public speaking, consulting, coaching, workshops, and digital offers. If my book is written and published correctly, I'll never be in a position again where I'll have to start from scratch within my business.

How can people connect with you?

I can be found at woostermediabooks.com and on Instagram @patriciawooster.

IF YOU PRIORITIZE CHARACTER, ABUNDANCE AND PROSPERITY FOLLOW, AND THE TREASURES OF YOUR LIFE ARE PASSED SEAMLESSLY TO OTHERS—EVEN IN YOUR LEGACY.

Tamra Andress

CHAPTER 3

MADE FOR MORE BY TAMRA ANDRESS

Surrounded by forty-plus fourth-quarter women in a room, all eyes were on me. I explained the diagnosis behind her death and proceeded to read the eulogy of a woman I had the privilege of calling my Nana. One by one, these women came to share with me not their condolences but instead their memories of her. At this session of life and location, a senior citizens apartment complex, death was no rare occasion, no matter how unexpected it was for us. They spoke of her stylish fashion sense and kindness, her smile, and her natural beauty. They spoke of her little idiosyncrasies and passions and how she never met a stranger. They spoke of her vibrancy and cheer. Not a word was mentioned about her profession or life's résumé.

I sat enamored and grateful. Hearing the legacy of a woman I had no clue had impacted so many simply by being herself. The tombstone moment of my life, which was the trajectory shift of my journey, merely five years before this moment, resurfaced again with refreshed and greater meaning.

I would not be listed as an "entrepreneur" on this side of heaven and surely not thereafter. So are my pursuits in tandem with my life's higher calling? Do I show up, in my intended purpose, despite a business card, despite a job title, despite a 401(k) or résumé-building agenda? My answer used to be no. It used to be fixated on the accolades and awards, the recognition, and the labels.

I was twenty-nine, working sixty-to-seventy-hour workweeks with a recently weaned nine-month-old little girl and a rambunctious one-year-old son. As the proud, not-so-humble CEO of two companies (a local and online brick and mortar and a global product-based company), I was living the fast-paced hustle-hard lifestyle, waiting for my phone to ding with new sales. My life was fixated on the American Dream that our coined "Barbie and Ken" lifestyle was accomplishing at a supersonic yet superficial pace. With blinders on my "entrepreneurial dream," I was sacrificing everything else—even my integrity.

After a twelve-hour day outside of the house, I expected to snuggle my littles when I got home. But instead, when I pulled into the driveway and saw my picturesque family hanging with the neighbors, my barely waddling daughter ran in the opposite direction of my arms. My gut twinged. My head spun. My heart sank. Was this the life I wanted? Was this the pace I desired? Detached from my husband, I went inside to be alone. And within the weeks to come, my non-anticipated quarter-life crisis led to the semi-forced release of both of my companies and the identity to which I had clung for over a decade.

Little white lies, both self-inflicted and societally deposited, led to shame-filled moments in the mirror and suicidal thoughts. But the whispers within my soul, the covenant promise of my husband, the children who dried my tears, and our intimate Father in heaven reminded me of the etched tombstone I would one day have:

Loving wife and mother, daughter and sister,
friend and Child of God.

My rat wheel had stopped, and I had a moment to reframe what fulfillment and life were all about. Priorities shifted. Old suppressing coping mechanisms were replaced with healthy, life-giving habits. New relationships emerged with rooted influence and wisdom. Therapists reframed my limiting beliefs, greatest fears, and past traumas. My marriage and home became a center of love and renewed connection. Intimacy was reestablished with my mirror moments. I was baptized, literally and figuratively, in the newness of my being. "What do you do?" was replaced with "What are you passionate about?" And for the first time in my life, I was fully seen and fully known, with an invigorated desire to serve others the same platter of life that had been gifted to me.

There are many beautiful (and painful) parts to this story. Details that we could sit sipping coffee over for hours to come. But the one area I want to emphasize for you here right now is the beautiful commitment we've been given, that He will make all things new and use all things for good and for His glory.

No trial, no tribulation, no test will go unmarked as worthless. Failures are just learning lessons and milestones for your emerging greatness. And while your dreams and aspirations may include financial blessings, it's not the focal point of your existence; after all, you can't take a hearse to heaven, just as my Nana couldn't take her stockpile of cash in her jewelry box. If you prioritize character, abundance and prosperity follow, and the treasures of your life are passed seamlessly to others—even in your legacy.

What is your *why* or purpose for your business?

As I reemerged from a three-year sabbatical and played the most difficult CEO role on the globe—chief estate officer, aka stay-at-home mom—I had a new sense of assurance in my calling. I had never lost the deep sense of knowing that I was made for more. Motherhood saved my life, after all. However, during that season, I also spent my time getting to know who I was made to be through the lens of whose I was claimed by (God). And through multiple immersive programs, including my ordination and ministers licensing, I had a fresh perspective on not only the *why* but the *how* I was intended to live out my purpose. The mind, body, soul, and Holy Spirit alignment zone became my consistent daily routine. Focusing on mental and physical health, emotional intelligence, meditation, worship, and relational communication, I was able to discover the abundance and prosperity I had been restlessly seeking. My *why* is to share, teach, free, and propel others into their truest sense of being, which develops their brand and business seamlessly thereafter.

What are the biggest mistakes you see new entrepreneurs making?

Aspiring and established dreamers and entrepreneurs regularly seek my support in business development and enhancement without emphasizing their personal need for internal growth. External desires, often carnal, plague their perspective on growth and strategy. Pursuing their dreams, no different than I did in my twenties, they exist in overdrive, overwhelm, and overcommitment. In my self-discovery and educational investigations of highly impactful individuals, I found external achievements and even tangible wealth to be of no value to their mission and no restraint to their expansion.

The definition of "success" is variable, and ultimately, it's the Ikigai that proves to be the zone that most miss the mark on every single time. Ikigai is a Japanese philosophy meaning "reason for being and path for fulfillment." Your zone of abundant existence is established within the connection of what you love, what you are good at, what you can be valued and paid for, and what the world needs. In this flow state, you experience internal peace so you can serve, love, and grow others from a place of wholeness. You've heard the phrase "Hurt people hurt people." Entrepreneurship is not for us. It's for others, and it's the most beautiful gift we give when operating from a place of alignment. As I'm sure you know firsthand, this expedition is not for the faint of heart. And therefore, just as we steward our time, we must steward our talents too—for our tombstones will be the seal of our life's relational roles, not our résumés. So our priority must be our sense of well-being before building a business that will inevitably have cracks due to the fractured human running it.

Which activities do you perform that generate the majority of your revenue?

What is revenue, after all? I know we're all on hyperdrive toward the dollar signs, but have you considered this question fully as you build your business? Revenue is a measure of income, and my heart for entrepreneurs and all humans is to exist in a state of overflow rather than overwhelm. When measurable metrics are the only premise of business, failure and shame have a tricky way of showing up regularly. If your mindset shifted in the conversation of revenue, and if money was freely coming to you and through you because of your abundant state of being, then revenue wouldn't be finite and could be measured on a multitude of levels, love and fulfillment included. But since you likely are wanting dollar signs here, I'll tell you the greatest impact is always with H2H transformation. As a friend and fellow entrepreneur, Joshua B. Lee, teaches, it's no longer a B2B or B2C transaction that generates revenue; instead, it's a human-to-human (H2H) and, I like to say, heart-to-heart exchange of value. My one-on-one coaching to date has provided me the ability to hire four full-time team members, covering overhead expenditures and savings for four to six months (in case I need some personal refuel to professionally serve—remember alignment is critical). Five-figure investments for four-month mentorships and annual masterminds provide the foundation for our business expansion.

How have you diversified your revenue streams within your business?

Diversification, as in any financial portfolio, is critical. Through memberships, group and one-on-one mentorships, podcast features, international retreats, conferences, one-off workshops, and VIP days, our company offers a multitude of access points to generate revenue and diversify our talents and interests while providing solutions to our community's needs.

Again, we could break this down to the alignment conversation too, which takes revenue to a deeper level of conversation and greater opportunity of wealth. After all, wealth is more than just a dollar sign. It includes all seven fruits of the spirit: love, joy, peace, forbearance, kindness, goodness, faithfulness, gentleness, and self-control (Galatians 5:22–23). By this measure, my Nana was the richest person I know.

As a way to capture these revelations for life abundance and a truly rich experience, I cultivated what I call the Joy Zone. This suits the entrepreneur, no different than the corporate exec, and even the stay-at-home mom simultaneously. Understanding the Joy Zone will keep you personally diversified so you can increase your capacity for business trajectory too.

The Joy Zone:

1. Heart: I explore and hold tight to my self-identity and deeper emotional awareness, connection, and love through the lens of God (Colossians 3:1–4).
2. Health: I love my body and treat it as a holy temple to support my greatest calling in longevity and with endurance and strength (1 Corinthians 6:19–20).
3. Head: My mental health is a priority, and by wearing my helmet of salvation, I crush limiting beliefs and enemy tactics to control my mind (Romans 12:2).

4. Home: My marriage covenant and children are my nucleus and have my primary and intentional focus and love (Galatians 2:24).
5. Handbag: Serving a prosperous and abundant God, my finances are overflowing and tithing is an honor (Deuteronomy 8:18).

What is your biggest day-to-day struggle in running your business?

Shiny-light syndrome. There are so many incredible dreamers, movers, shakers, and makers creating every single day and offering beautiful opportunities to grow, both personally and professionally. I love social media and use it as a tactic to spread joy and activate purpose in the lives of others, so I have to safe harbor my newsfeeds to stay focused on my primary goal and the people who are providing influence and teaching. While we often mindlessly spend time in these places, it's critical to realize that nothing we do is mindless. Our eyes, ears, and spirits are subconsciously receiving, ideating, and depositing into our soul and processing center. Shiny lights—glitz, glam, and guilty pleasures included—can be the bane of our existence and the destruction of our being, leading to brand and business failure.

What have you found helps with blending your personal and professional life?

By now, if you haven't caught on that my life's experience proves this crucial awareness of enmeshment, we should jump on a call. But I think you are smarter than that. So to seal the concept, let me give you a visual to grasp hold of. Being aligned vertically first and foremost (personally) in mind, body, soul, and spirit will allow you to horizontally serve holistically and openhanded without need for reciprocity. In this state of being, prosperity is inevitable.

What self-care, routines, and habits do you have to maintain good health?

These are my seven secrets to living a day of fulfillment and whole health:

1. Worship: prayer, gratitude, music
2. Workout: move the body
3. Words: the Word and devotional time
4. Warmth: get those kisses from your spouse, kiddos, and loved ones (pet slobber welcomed too)
5. Wins: set your day up to win, calendar design, and reflection and celebration of the win (no matter how big or small)
6. Write: the emails, the texts, the notes before distractions
7. Winks: staying woke to the "not so coincidental" coincidences within your day

Sometimes people put such emphasis on their morning routine, which I am absolutely a 4:00 to 5:00 A.M. start of day kind of girl. However, I think people often can get stuck on checking all the boxes without staying present in the growth and the becoming of the process. I allow free flow on these items within my day, keeping the emphasis on the God winks He is providing in the midst, all day long. I notice my most productive days include all of these elements, and the days they are not all touched, I lack a sense of fulfillment.

What is the most worthwhile investment you have made for your business?

It has hands down been the incredible people I've brought on board to share in the vision of global kingdom impact. Relational strength, deep connection, and inner-circle guidance have been the backbone to our team's seemingly quick three-year propel.

In my previous achievement-driven perspective, I had to be the one in control, doing all the things and maintaining every role as if I were some kind of superhuman. I didn't often take advice. I went off gut feelings (which I later discovered wasn't intuition but purely selfish and emotionally driven). And well, you know how that story ended. So as I emerged into entrepreneurship again, I knew relationships, with connection, intimacy, and vulnerability, would be the building blocks to harmony, health, and wealth. This revelation was not a light-switch experience, no matter how many experts or coaches told me to do this or books suggested it. The unlock was my internal nucleus prioritization of relationship—my personal home. As my marriage strengthened and I learned to stop trying to "wear the pants," I realized wearing a dress was way more my style and freedom existed in the symbiotic existence rather than a push-pull, give-and-take, hierarchical structure . . . plus, there was a lot more peace and a whole heck of a lot more fun. And so I took what I activated inside and utilized it in my business.

If you walk into our office (no different than our home), you sense joy, not only from our rainbow brand and palm tree green space but because of the laughter, light, and love that ruminates. The more I release what is outside of my zone of genius, the more I can emphasize and focus on what God has uniquely equipped me to do. And because my capacity expands when I'm operating inflow, I can be more in tune with the emotions and desires of those around me and become a stronger, more empathetic, and motivated leader. Additionally, dissecting a fail-forward learning experience and celebrating a big win as a team rather than solo is much more enjoyable with others who can fully appreciate the blood, sweat, and tears that went into it all.

I get it, though. Team building can seem scary. It can feel like you're increasing your expenses, oftentimes before your revenue, which doesn't seem like a very effective business strategy. However, there are several ways to approach your team build, which can ease your hesitancy. The first priority is perspective on hiring and growing a team. People are valued investments, not expenses. By adopting this mindset, you tend to nurture the human rather than criticize the cost.

In transparency, I eased my way into this mindset shift. My first hire wasn't a paid position. For a year and a half, it was a shared partnership through an emerging friendship. We leaned on one another by tapping into our unique gifts and talents. The relationships organically systemized a growth model as we developed the shared vision and energy surged around the expansion of our plan and the freedom of our roles. My friend quit her full-time job and became my first full-time hire, helping to further establish a strong, rooted company culture and brand that has become the magnetic force to our clients and community. One by one, we brought in people to the team who fulfilled our needs and their calling simultaneously. The support of my spouse and family in this process has been instrumental as a backbone to this body and the consistent reminder of my *why*. While some believe "you don't take work home," we strongly disagree and make sure home goes with us everywhere we go, even at work. By relying on the family unit and considering it no different than a team, my children have already taken a strong passion toward entrepreneurship, relational strengths and weaknesses, and the power of pursuing their passion versus their "job." Our team is a family, and our family is a team. And families grow in love. Our vision is still expanding . . . and so is our team.

Here are some critical areas of focus in the team-building process to help nurture a healthy environment and successful outcomes:

- Allow your team members to curate their job descriptions—this instills their success and passionate desired input into their role daily.
- Invest in further education in their areas of expertise and passion, developing their zone of genius—complacency in knowledge will create stagnancy in your growth trajectory.

- Tap into personal goals just as much as you emphasize professional ones. Partner with them in those success strategies and accountability.
- Offer incentive-based pay paralleled to salary (everyone has different motivations).
- Start your week off together in team meetings that help curate the energy for the week ahead.
- Pray together without ceasing!
- Cut loose together—build bonds besides business. Remember, family first.

If you lost everything today, what would you do for the next thirty days to generate income?

We have moved on from coffee at this point in our relationship and are now speaking at the teatime evening hour where I'd love to indulge in this conversation with you, for this question probes philosophy more than it does strategy if you're aligned in your being. Because in that place, you cannot lose what the world does not own. And you have been bought with a price that no person could pay you. But I'll comply to support those in need of a business build and strategy; after all, I am a purpose activator, and business coach has been my title for years now.

Earlier, we discussed the path to fulfillment and reason for being, known as the Ikigai. Let's circle back to its imagery and robust understanding so that you can sit with me in all of my emotions and thought patterns toward this critical question. I would first spend the day dissecting the diagram (google image search "Ikigai" for quick reference) designed to snapshot your current placement within your awareness of your reason for being. The Ikigai exists in the combination of: what you love, what the world needs, what you can be paid for, and what you are good at—all layered together with your passion, mission, profession, and vocation. If you teeter within a few, you exist dissatisfied in the following zones:

- The zone between passion and profession without mission and vocation = satisfaction, but the feeling of uselessness.
- The zone between passion and mission without profession and vocation = delight and fullness, but not wealth.
- The zone between mission and vocation without passion and profession = excitement and complacency, but the sense of uncertainty.
- The zone between vocation and profession without passion and mission = comfortable, but a feeling of emptiness.

Upon completion and recognition of fulfillment in all four categories, I would confirm my marketing strategy in the vulnerability of who I am authentically rather than what the world expects me to be. What others need from me and how I can create value does not stem from a false highlight reel, but instead yearns for deep connection, relatability, and access to transformation. I would lean into high-ticket, experiential one-on-one coaching in order to help others break through paralleled experiences.

Often, people are unsure of their value, worth, or legitimacy in coaching based on lack of certifications and imposter syndrome. Let me help validate you real quick if you've ever experienced these suppressing ideations: You have made it this far. You were born for such a time as this. And not one other human being on the planet knows exactly what you know. By not serving others from this place of knowledge and wisdom, you are blocking their blessings because you have the key to their "aha moment" of freedom.

I would start locally, building in-person relationships, and focus the remainder of my first week on social proofing my concept, adding value organically and freely, and utilizing the power of video testimonials. My next week would focus on sharing that content and having those first week's people connect me to others who may want and need a similar transformation. I would create a Dream 100 list (25 people you directly know, 25 people they know, 25 people you indirectly know, and 25 people you could only dream of connecting with). I would set a goal to connect, text, call, email, DM, or voice memo three people from each list per day. Setting the SMARTest goal of signing at least two new clients by the end of the month at $10,000 each with a nurturing plan for all of the contacts I have touched base with.

I'm sure you've heard of the SMART goals by now, but the EST is what will generate the next pathway of profitability:

- E = Evaluate
- S = Share
- T = Tailor

Think of the EST being the answer to the question "What now?" You've achieved the goal, but momentum halts if you stop there. Without a goal or follow-up plan, we will be back at square one to this question. So you must look back in evaluation, share your discoveries with those who are helping propel your vision, and tailor your next SMART goal to these discoveries. And of course, activate again.

Through all of this, I would emphasize the Joy Zone to exist as a Joyful Entrepreneur (this is my eight-week coaching program) impacting all of those you are called to serve, displaying the fruits of the spirit and claiming the truth to your tombstone.

How can people connect with you?

I can be found on Instagram @tamra.andress and by email at tamra@tamraandress.com.

AS A NEW ENTREPRENEUR, CONCENTRATING ON YOUR NETWORK FIRST MEANS BUILDING A BUSINESS WITH SUSTAINABILITY AND LONGEVITY.

Kimberly Beer

CHAPTER 4

EVERYTHING YOU NEED IS WITHIN YOU BY KIMBERLY BEER

What if I told you that you already have everything you need to be successful as an entrepreneur?

The first time someone said this to me, I sat back in my chair shaking my head. It was during an impromptu coffee shop coaching session with a mentor I highly respected. *No way*, I thought, *I need* a lot *of stuff to be successful—most notably, more money.* Also, new software, a different camera, maybe a business partner, and this training/certification course I'd been eyeing as the way to convince my clients (and myself) I knew what I was doing. The list was endless.

At the time, I'd been doing the entrepreneur thing in the form of a marketing design and consulting firm for twelve years. I had gotten damn good at being scrappy. It was my second act as a business owner, the first act having ended in bankruptcy court. This time, I'd done it smarter and better. I consistently supported myself. It wasn't always pretty, but there was food on the table, a roof over my head, and a business that was growing. During the recession, which ended right before the "question" came up, I had a close call with foreclosure paperwork and I'd experienced the less-than-glamorous activity of reclaiming my Jeep from the repo lot. I'd gotten through to the other side with my business, home, and car, but it was painful and embarrassing.

During those twelve years, there were many mornings the woman I faced in the mirror mouthed, "What the hell do you think you're doing?" As I'd turn my back on her and walk the five feet to my home office, she'd say, "Get a *real* job." I ignored her because I was committed to never seeing the inside of a corporate cubicle again. I could do without for one. More. Day. I gave myself kudos for my scrappiness and went to work.

The mentor's question burned at me. I couldn't shake the ramifications of "what *if* I did have everything I needed to be successful?" More importantly, how did I define success? I vividly remember pondering these concepts as I cleaned stalls—an activity that is 10 percent cleaning and 90 percent deep thought processing. Later, during an after-chore walk in the woods, I sat down on Mother Earth and opened myself up. I allowed the possibility to enter my heart. *What if I already have everything I needed to be successful?* If that coach could believe it, and she was a successful entrepreneur by all standards, then what was stopping me? I took stock:

- I had inherited an expansive piece of land but not the knowledge or resources to manage it well. Yet I had figured out how to turn the financial burden of caring for it into multiple income streams that not only supported the land but brought in a growing profit.
- I had been bankrupt. Yet I walked away with a better understanding of how money worked, and when faced with being an entrepreneur during a recession, I had stumbled, but I did not go down for the count. Instead, I had scrambled back to my feet, better than ever.
- I had fought with depression, anxiety, and stress. Yet I had figured out how to make a workable peace with each and still function and thrive—even on days when my internal demons were screaming for my focus.

- I was making a difference every day in the lives of my clients. I celebrated with them the successes I helped create. Others recognized it too and sought me out as a creative consultant.

One other thing was crystal clear: I am resilient. To be honest, that was the realization that surprised me. My family had always considered me lazy and too soft for the harsh world. I was labeled flighty and inconsistent by corporate employers. Several therapists had felt I shouldn't walk through this life without the support of medication, which made me feel like a zombie.

So, where did the resilience come from? As if on cue, the neigh of a horse in the distance caught my attention. *Yes,* I thought. *There.*

The wind rustled the trees. *Yes, there, too.*

All around me since I arrived on this planet were examples of resilience and success. The horses in the pasture, the cows that grazed on the hillside, the wildlife in the timber around me, the goats in the paddock, and the crops in the field were all examples of how to be successful. They didn't need the latest software. They didn't need a new camera, they didn't use money to buy their way into happiness, they didn't need a certificate to prove they were capable. They needed no one's approval. They simply accessed their unique gift to be who they needed to be in the moment. That was all they needed to get to the next moment, quite successfully. If that success was over-the-top . . . well, that brought more joy to the moment.

In my time on this ranch, I have been witness to devastation and rebirth in endless cycles. The important thing to note is that rebirth *always* comes in some form or another. Nature always finds a way. Nature is creative, resourceful, bountiful, and resilient. Unfortunately, being removed from the land means many people see nature as fragile. Don't believe it for a moment—nature is tougher than you know and far more infinite than you can imagine. When you work alongside it, you see that in real terms every day.

As entrepreneurs, we are given, by our very nature, everything we need to find a way. We are creative, resourceful, bountiful, and resilient. We are not fragile—although we may appear that way at times. We are far more infinite. The thing we lose touch with is how to connect with ourselves, our creativity, our resourcefulness, our values, and our innate gifts—and, more importantly, we don't know how to trust that connection and those gifts even when we find them.

When I was asked that ever-important question, I did not trust myself to have the answers. I did not see myself as infinitely capable. All I saw were holes in my world that needed to be filled, and I was stuffing them with anything and everything I could find. It worked, but it didn't work well. At the encouragement of my mentor and her thought-provoking question, I took a leap of faith that day in the woods and began the process of learning to trust myself. It was the best business decision I have ever made.

Since I became an entrepreneur, I have helped thousands of people with their marketing and business plans. Many come to me overwhelmed, even distraught, over their business. They feel like failures—like their business isn't measuring up, or they are doing something wrong. Some feel they are missing a key ingredient. They are looking at the holes in their world. They are always hopeful I will hand them the perfect answer, the entrepreneurial secret they've not been privy to—yet.

I have since discovered that a different business plan, a new ad collateral, a redesigned website, a different set of AdWords, or different email marketing software was not the solution for most of my clients. The fact they were stretching into these areas wasn't bad or wrong, and it addressed a need, but that need was an extension of a symptom, not the underlying issue. If you don't address the underlying issue, the overwhelm and failure will continue despite the plan, ad, website, or software.

When I dig deep into the client's business, the underlying issue usually leads right back to the person running the business and their limiting beliefs, unfinished business, or unconscious scripts that dictate their mindset. It leaves them with a narrowed vision that only sees holes and not the material already in their possession that will fill those holes.

This is where my answer to that coaching question came into play and I embarked on a process that is continuing to provide growth to my business and personal life. I signed up for an intensive training program with that mentor who opened my eyes to all this possibility and began adding new and needed skills to my tool kit. I studied, learned, expanded, and, most importantly, worked on clearing my own limiting beliefs and unfinished business. I started rewriting and rewiring those unconscious scripts that caused me to react instead of respond. I reached out to my ranch, to nature, to my horses, and to my creative muse to help me make positive shifts that cleared those underlying issues.

I then grew new programs and services into my existing business by merging a unique blend of the wisdom I'd gathered from psychology, art, business, and agriculture.

In doing so, I moved from servicing my clients to empowering them. I went from being just another consultant in their businesses to igniting the fuel in their creative entrepreneurial gas tank. I took the things that had been supporting me all along—my ranch, horses, nature, my experience, my wisdom, my creativity, my gift of seeing the details and the thirty-thousand-foot view at one time—and lent them to my clients in a way that could unlock their unique awareness and gifts. I stopped trying to do business for them and started teaching and inspiring them to do business with and as themselves.

Today, my mission is built around helping other mission-driven entrepreneurs connect to what they need to reach their dreams and then become joyfully sustainable for as long as they want to be in business. This starts with connecting them to themselves and their innate gifts. Then, I empower them to build on that connection—to develop self-compassion and self-trust. I want them to know that they already know the secret—and they didn't learn it in any marketing book or business-planning manual. Everything in their life has prepared them for this moment—and this moment will prepare them for the next.

The ranch, nature, horses especially, and art all play a role in the services I offer. All of these are creative endeavors. Entrepreneurship is all about creation. The ranch and nature offer inspiration that connects us to ourselves at a level you just can't reach in a boardroom. Horses, who long ago cocreated a covenant with humankind, offer their giant hearts and present-moment wisdom to bring us into contact with that inspiration. They call us on our bullshit in a way only the equine soul is capable of. Horses also drive us to reach deep into the well of our souls where the true answers to anything and everything we need lay waiting. Art and creativity allow us to draw those answers and knowledge into the physical world where we can access it, use it, and expand on it.

Not everyone is as blessed as I am to have all this waiting right outside their office door, which is why I offer on-site journeys at the ranch where clients can get away from their businesses long enough to build a better mindset. They leave the ranch in contact with themselves and their businesses—and empowered with the tools they need and now know how to use—to meet the challenges that come their way.

As for me, this shift has been nothing but positive for my entrepreneurial growth. I have continued an upward trajectory that shows no indication of slowing down. I am excited about the future. Although I am entirely prepared to be scrappy at any given moment, the woman in the mirror is now proud of who she sees each morning.

What is your *why* or purpose for your business?

My *why* is to make a difference for my clients. In tangible terms, that means helping entrepreneurs move away from overwhelm, frustration, and fear while moving them toward growth, empowerment, and success they can sustain long term. But it's also much more than that. Making a difference is my highest value—it's the thing that most drives me. When I'm making a difference, I feel alive, impassioned, and joyful. That energy is the space I want to be in as much as possible, so I created a career for myself where I can bask in it every day.

What are the biggest mistakes you see new entrepreneurs making?

Not spending enough time and energy on building their network. Your network is the heartbeat of your business growth. It's where impactful marketing and growth take place. It's where you can go when you have challenges, problems, or just need a boost.

I have two networks I utilize. One is my Sustainability Squad, and the other is my Joint Venture Team. They are equally important and vital to building a sustainable business.

My Sustainability Squad is focused on my growth as an entrepreneur and human being. It includes six groups of people:

1. Mentors who help me by sharing their experience and knowledge.
2. Teachers from whom I learn vital skills.
3. Coaches who help me realize my potential.
4. Advisors who have specialized knowledge I need access to.
5. Sponsors who represent me when opportunities arise.
6. Cheerleaders who celebrate me no matter what.

Some of the roles on my Sustainability Squad are provided pro bono, like mentors, sponsors, and cheerleaders. In other roles, I will pay either for their services, like coaches, or for a product they offer, like advisors (for example, an insurance agent or lawyer). Regardless, it's my job to build and maintain good relationships with each member of my squad so I have easy access anytime I face a challenge or want to expand on a growth opportunity.

My Joint Venture Team is focused on growing my business reach. I consider—and treat—people on my JV Team just like a business partner. There is a growth benefit for both parties built into the relationship from step one. I expect my JV Team members to carry half the weight of our endeavors and bring a whole benefit with them. For example, suppose I partner with a new business owner who is seeking to build their list by being introduced to my wider influence. In that case, I expect that business owner to bring a skill or knowledge my clients will find useful and beneficial. All JV partners should equally share responsibility and expenses, and both should reap benefits from the relationship. My JV Team includes complementary businesses, influencers, experts, and sometimes even my best customers and sponsors.

As a new entrepreneur, concentrating on your network first means building a business with sustainability and longevity. You spread the work of marketing and growth among many minds while being the guiding force for your vision. Along the way, you pay it back and forward by being part of that larger ecosystem that supports us all.

How have you diversified your revenue streams within your business?

I have three distinct business income streams: my ranch, consulting business, and photography business. Each of those businesses has income streams of its own.

When I took over management of the ranch in 1999, we were strictly a cow-calf operation. If that market suffered, we suffered. But we had investments that could help us through any bad situation. When my mother passed away in 2005, those investments were cashed out and distributed between my sister and me so that I couldn't depend on family anymore. I had to change my management practice. Plus, I had a growing marketing business off-farm that needed attention. Today, our income is derived from a very small cow-calf operation and land leases for row crops, pasture, hunting, and motorcycle races. The ranch plays a big part in my marketing and consulting business by providing the backdrop for our Journeys program, workshops, and retreats.

I derive income from consulting, coaching, speaking, teaching, and some production work in my consulting business. Each activity feeds off the other activities. For example, my speaking income stream introduces me to consulting and coaching clients who come to my classes and technical courses. This business ties in with the ranch for our Journeys programs, where my entrepreneurial clients come to the ranch for intensive multiday business-building workshops. This is where my heart is the happiest: combining my love of nature and horses with my passion for helping entrepreneurs. I am expanding this arm of my business.

I am also a professional photographer. I started this arm of my business because I wanted good images to use for my clients' marketing pieces back when I did design work. A lot of my work is done with equine-related businesses. I was good at capturing images of horses and their people, and I love doing it. Through serendipity and some hard work, I got involved in partnering with the Equine Photographers Network (EPNet), hosting a retreat for photographers at a big ranch in Wyoming. I had so much fun photographing horses day and night, out in nature, and with amazing equestrian models that I'd almost forgotten about the paycheck coming my way. When it arrived, I was speechless—I could have that much fun and make a pile of money? Sign me up! I'm now involved in several workshops and retreats beyond EPNet. This income stream fills in my summer months when the ranch is running on autopilot, when many of my consulting clients are rotating through their vacations, and when the weather in Missouri is, well, less than desirable. I can be out west where it's cool, teaching and leading photographers with my retreat business partners. Plus, most of the photographers who come to our events are entrepreneurs, so this income stream feeds the consulting business.

What is one of your greatest failures that ultimately led to success?

First, I believe failure is just a step on the way to success. All of my failures have led to success. Sometimes the success is saying, "I'm not going to do that again!" But I digress. I would consider one of my greatest failures my trip through bankruptcy court for my first business. I made so many mistakes. I listened to the advice of people who had no business knowledge, I borrowed too much money, I tried to buy my way past the competition, I had a business partner I should have sent packing long before I did. I was young with too much hubris to admit I had no idea how cash flow worked in a business. I didn't know how much work a business entailed or how deeply my depression might impact my ability to run a business. It was one of the worst moments in my life when I had to admit defeat in this business. And the worst part: most of the money I'd borrowed and would never be paid back came from my family. Ouch.

I can remember the bankruptcy judge asking me, "If I were to forgive your debt, what will you do to never, ever end up in front of me again?"

I responded, "I will never own another business." At the time, I meant it. I'd lost friendships. I'd hurt my family financially, I'd failed my clients and employees, I was in a heavy depression that felt like it would never lift.

I immediately found a corporate job and went back to a cubicle. I cannot tell you definitively what the company I worked for did to this day. I hated that job from day one. Nothing I did made it better—not the money, not the quick promotions, not even the nice people I worked with. I was twenty-seven years old and felt like I had no future. In just over a year, I quit and went back to college to finish my degree in creative writing. Not two months into my return semester, I was smoking (yes, I've since quit!) and hovering around an ashtray outside an event with a group of other smokers. A woman in the group was complaining that her graphic designer had just up and quit and left them without anyone to do their magazine. I said, "Um, I'm a graphic designer."

Although it would be another year before Midnight Productions, Inc. would officially be born, and several after that before it became a corporate entity, my reentry back into entrepreneurship happened at that moment, and I haven't looked back since. I took the hard lessons my first business had taught me and applied them. I got real help from people who knew about small businesses. I didn't try to do it all at once, but instead I concentrated on building a business that would grow on a solid foundation. I took classes, studied, went to seminars, found mentors, did anything and everything I could to learn about—and execute—being a successful small business owner. I was humble. I knew it wasn't going to be easy, and I was okay with that.

I wouldn't trade one step of this journey—even the bankruptcy—for a different outcome. I needed every one of those lessons to arrive at where I am at today. And I will need every lesson I learn today and tomorrow to arrive at where I'm going next week, next month, and next year. I welcome the successes and the failures because they are both huge opportunities.

What hard lessons have you learned that could have been avoided?

The hardest lesson I had in business—and in life—was understanding how much I get in my own way. I had a harsh and stressed childhood. It left me with many limiting beliefs, unfinished business, and scripts that ran in my head on autoplay. One of those scripts was, "You have to work hard to earn money." This script tag-teamed with a limiting belief that I was lazy. Plus, I had unfinished business with my family members who had handed me these introjects. There were things I needed to say but couldn't, because these people were either gone from the planet or no longer in my life. All of this was a recipe for business disaster—I felt I had to bust my butt eighteen hours a day to deserve my paycheck and prove I wasn't lazy to people who weren't even in my life.

This was when I met a woman named Melisa Pearce, who introduced me to the practice of Gestalt. Melisa runs a successful business called Touched by a Horse in Colorado. She is a Gestalt psychotherapist, and she has developed a method that pairs Gestalt practices with horses to help people overcome limiting beliefs, complete unfinished business, and change their lives.

Gestalt is a psychotherapy model that believes each of us is born fully capable and whole. Traumas—both big and small—can temporarily fracture that wholeness until we resolve the energetic charge around them. Where talk therapy is passive and guided, Gestalt is active and accessible. Gestalt happens in experiential activities that bring a person into contact with themselves in a way that can resolve the trauma and remove its energetic charge forever for them.

Melisa had hired me to photograph and film some of her work to show how her horses supported and deepened her Gestalt therapy practice. At the time, she was at the beginning of developing a program to train others in her method. I was a rebounding entrepreneur trying to build a creative marketing business. From the moment I watched the first piece of Gestalt work, I knew I needed exactly what I had witnessed: to be released from the energetic bonds of my past. Melisa is, to this day, one of my most cherished clients and one of my most important mentors.

Ten years later, I am working toward incorporating Gestalt into all the programs I create for entrepreneurs. I have experienced myself and seen in countless others the massive shift Gestalt can make. My only wish is that I would have met Melisa sooner—and started living Gestalt sooner—so I could have gotten out of my way faster!

If you lost everything today, what would you do for the next thirty days to generate income?

First, I'd reach out to my network. When everything seems lost, it's easy to forget we are all connected through a magical supportive ecosystem. Whenever I have faced a challenge, financial or otherwise, my network is there to help me find my way, which is why I believe everyone, but especially entrepreneurs, should place network building, maintenance, and growth at the top of their list of things to do. I would first look for people willing to lend me a helping hand and a soft place to land. Then, I'd look for people who will pay for or refer me to people who will pay for my expertise, experience, and creativity. Once I gained back some balance, I'd set my sights on the next great adventure and reach out to my network for support, investments, and joint ventures to thrive in that endeavor.

How can people connect with you?

I can be found at kim@bemorebusiness.com.

I WILL ALWAYS INVEST IN THE BEST TEACHER AND BE THE BEST STUDENT IF IT WILL MAKE ME A GOOD TEACHER TO SOMEONE ELSE.

Tina Booker

CHAPTER 5

NEW BEGINNINGS BY TINA BOOKER

I knew very early on in life that I would not work forever to get someone else rich. I didn't want to be an employee forever. I knew I wanted to own a business of my own. I just didn't know how it would happen. Knowing this from a young age made it easy to retire from the New York City Department of Corrections to start my journey toward freedom. I was released from this job after twenty years of working in the toughest jail in the United States. You may have heard of it. It was Rikers Island.

I was very inspired by many people in my life who started their own businesses. I come from a long line of women entrepreneurs. They had no idea how much I watched and paid attention to what they were doing. This started for me at age four, which was when I began to understand ownership. My great-uncle had a bar in Wildwood, New Jersey. My family would visit him during the summer. He would come out from behind the bar and give me a small paper bag full of quarters to play the pinball machine. Once I used those quarters, he would give me more money for my older cousins to walk me to the beach to enjoy the boardwalk and rides. As a little girl, I knew my great-uncle was his own boss who always seemed to have a lot of money for me.

My dad's eldest sister owned and operated a daycare center in Brooklyn, New York, named Kiddie Academy. My mom also worked for her for a short time until she decided to open a daycare of her own. She partnered with one of my dad's younger sisters to open a daycare in Brooklyn. My mom eventually pulled out, but my aunt remained the owner and employed other family members, including my mom, who stayed on board as an educator until we relocated south for a few years. The daycare center was located in the storefront below our apartment. They all made sure we knew that it was our family business. We always got away with a little more than the other children. Things like staying up at nap time were cool for me, or sitting in my aunt's office as she did payroll. It was amazing to spend every single day with so many family members.

I don't know how I knew that she owned the business at such a young age, but I did. I knew that she had the daycare, and my uncle owned the bar. I admired their cars and style of dress. They had the best of everything. Mink coats and Cadillacs. My aunt took me shopping when I got older and spent the summers with my dad. We would shop at Daffy's and eat at Red Lobster. In the '70s, I thought that was the life of rich people and I wanted to do what they did to have the money to get those nice things.

My family expanded by starting a private transportation business. They bused the children to the daycare and the local elementary schools. My daughter was fortunate enough to attend the daycare and get bused there daily before my aunt retired and closed the daycare. We had other family members who continued with the transportation services. My aunt went on to start her insurance broker business before retirement.

She was not the only example. My favorite person (other than my mom) was my Nanny, which was my mother's mom. When we relocated south, I witnessed how hard my grandmother worked. She lost her right hand in an accident at her job, so she was an amputee. However, her disability didn't stop her. She was a young widow with five children who had to hustle to pay the bills. Once she became a grandmother, she worked even harder. She relocated to Detroit, Michigan, where she opened a beauty supply store. She turned ownership over to my aunt and started selling antique goods well into her late seventies.

All of these important people in my life who were working hard in their businesses had a tremendous impact on me. Their work ethic and all the lessons I learned as a child stuck with me. Even when I was working as a corrections officer, I knew it was only a matter of time before following in their footsteps.

What is your *why* or purpose for your business?

The one thing that I will always live by is what my Nanny said to me as a young woman with so many dreams and aspirations: "Do what you love to do and work where you enjoy going to work." It's a disservice to work where you are not happy. Nothing good comes from it. Not for you or the employer. The *why* for me is really the *why not*. I am a black woman in America with an endless opportunity to show my family that nothing they've done was in vain.

I am proud to be blessed with gifts and talents that have turned a profit for me after working from the age of nineteen. I retired at forty-six years old to do what I love to do and not what I have to do to keep food on the table. I'm continuing my family's legacy of servicing people with love. *Love* is my motivator. I love to provide services that will help another family start their legacy. I love to inspire people, just as my grandmother did for me. I want to be there to encourage people to do what they love. I love to see happiness, especially if it's from one of my products or services.

What are the biggest mistakes you see new entrepreneurs making?

Not doing enough research for the prospective new business they want to start. Especially if they have little to no experience in the industry or the business they believe they want to create. These days, most new entrepreneurs are looking for microwave success. Often, they don't realize that successful companies with longevity don't happen overnight. You have to understand and truly know the pros and cons, the *wheres, whens, hows, whos, ins, outs, dos,* and *don'ts*. Especially the *why*. The only way to get those answers is to do your research. It will save a lot of time, frustration, and money.

You must be purposeful about your intentions to succeed at whatever you want to do in life. Being able to answer the questions about the purpose of your business says a lot about you. It's about understanding the needs of your customers and clients. If you don't even know the basic answers about them—such as, what do they like, how old are they, what's the demand for what they do—you're working backward. Without those answers, the business often goes under rather quickly.

Uncertainties are not good in business. If you have that gut feeling to wait, then lean into that feeling and *wait*! I'm a person of little to no patience. That's not a good trait to have in business. It will cause you to make irrational decisions just to get started. That's another mistake that entrepreneurs make: not giving themselves enough time to test the water.

For example, if you rent a space for a restaurant that sells all fried foods and sweets located between a gym, a yoga studio, and a bariatric clinic just because the space is available, then that's a terrible mistake. How is that going to work out? You can't break the lease just because you didn't take the time to research the best location for your business. These things happen more often than you think due to a lack of patience and market knowledge.

Starting small and growing consistently is the key. Many times, new entrepreneurs over-order products from vendors prior to researching the supply and demand for the product. Take advantage of sample orders and order in low quantities.

Social media is often misleading when it comes to the success of products and services. Seeing product ads and assuming they are selling a lot is a common mistake. Most of the time, it's just a lot of views or likes and minimal sales. They're often sitting on a pile of products, running ads to get rid of them, and putting out the perception that everyone is buying what they are selling. None of this is based on facts but on how they are putting themselves out there.

I also think new entrepreneurs don't respect experience enough. A person can be in the same business as you and have a track record that is longer. Don't look at them as just your competitor. They can be a great business model to follow or have as a mentor. Their mistakes can save you money, and their success can make you money. If they offer you advice, take it. Use what you can and leave what doesn't apply.

Which activities do you perform that generate the majority of your revenue?

Attending in-person events, engaging in community events, and livestreaming. Consumers are emotional buyers. Big advertisers have mastered tapping into the emotions of all of us as consumers. I am a hands-on person. I always want my consumers and supporters to feel my sincerity and appreciation. I like to converse with my customer base. It allows me to do my quality assurance even after a purchase. I find that doing giveaways during a livestream gets more people involved than normal. They end up purchasing what they wanted to win during the giveaway.

Being an e-commerce business and service provider, I treat my business as a brick and mortar. So, I ask myself, "What's going to make someone stop at my store (which is actually my social media account) as opposed to the store next door?" My answer to myself is to be personable and interactive. It has worked thus far with my business and my community activism.

The biggest misconception is that people with large followings are making the most money. Content is what makes you money. Being seen and interactive has never let me down. Treating your customers and clients with respect brings more sales. They will tell everyone else about you. I like to make my interactions and experience with my clients special. They know that every sale is important to me. Plus, they are not sympathetic buyers (the people who buy only because they're your friends or family). They buy from me because of my customer service and appreciation.

How have you diversified your revenue streams within your business?

Utilizing my mistakes and success to start an empowerment coaching business. I am empowering other women to do what they love to do and not what they have to do. In addition, I have a business division where I share my day-to-day life as an entrepreneur with my husband and routine through workbooks for other couples in business.

My love for entertainment and story sharing has allowed me to start a production company to produce a docuseries and a reality show. In addition, I've created long-term security through investments in the stock market.

What is one of your greatest failures that ultimately led to success?

When I had to close my café in Brooklyn ten years ago. I began to doubt everything I had ever done before it. I didn't think I would recover financially or emotionally. Success for me is never financial; it's having the ability to trust myself enough to either try again or do something different that will accomplish the goal I've envisioned.

What hard lessons have you learned that could have been avoided?

When we opened our café, we had no experience in the restaurant business or the business of being in business. It was an idea without a plan that went from a place to entertain to a full-service restaurant. We could have avoided losing the amount of money we did in the beginning by doing what all small business owners should do without exception: take the time to learn the business before you begin to invest your money.

What is your biggest day-to-day struggle in running your business?

Time management and staffing. Being an entrepreneur, along with the other things I am involved with, takes a lot of my time some days. Scheduling things that only I can do causes setbacks for not just me but also for others I may be collaborating with on another project that has nothing to do with my business. It could be for a non-for-profit project that's just as important. I am learning not to be apologetic for things I just can't do that will take me away from time that should be spent on my business. My spontaneity can be problematic. I can think of something and want to immediately execute it. However, just because I can do it doesn't mean that I should, especially if other people or my team have to alter plans and schedules to get it done.

The same thing goes for multitasking. I worked in fields where multitasking was part of my job. Now that I'm the boss, I have to constantly remind myself that I don't have to do that anymore. Taking on one task at a time has been difficult. However, I have started to adjust and have realized it's less stressful.

What have you found helps with blending your personal and professional life?

I find sharing parts of my personal life helps me with getting work done without neglecting my family, and getting them involved at times with the business is a fun way to ensure it doesn't feel like work. They're always down for it if they're going to have fun doing it while spending time together. For example, I can plan a couples retreat and incorporate a beauty day for the ladies with some of my cosmetic products that they may want to purchase for a dinner party planned during the retreat. Everyone wins. I have time with my hubby and make some money while providing another wife with what she needs for the evening.

I also like to share my faith and my community activism. Most people are shocked to hear I am a Christian pastor of a small ministry or that I'm the founder of a nonprofit organization. I love to find ways to give back through my businesses or share words of inspiration without offending any other religious belief. I am very passionate about the well-being of children and underserved communities. I have used and continue to use my platforms and my businesses to be a resource in many ways that have benefited families in need and inner-city youth and ministries as much as I can.

What self-care, routines, and habits do you have to maintain good health?

My self-care routines change periodically depending on what I feel I need to take care of, whether it's me, my family, or my community. One consistent thing is my fitness goals. I vowed to myself to never completely stop working out. After working in law enforcement and developing specific medical conditions, and having permanent injuries, I have to continue to give my body what it needs for it to keep working for me. In addition, I get professional counseling when things become overwhelming. I think it's important to take care of both your physical and mental health.

Devotional time is very important to me too. I have to start my day in my spiritual place of prayer, praise, reflections, and gratitude. It keeps me grounded and centered.

And let's not forget about travel. Vacations are a must. I have to take time for myself and my family. It reminds me of how blessed I am and why I do what I do.

What is the most worthwhile investment you have made for your business?

Investing in coaches and having mentors and counselors. Having professionals who can teach you the best strategies for your business and save you from making amateur mistakes is worth every penny if you get the results you were expecting and deserve.

The time I have invested in learning what's required for the things I need to reach my goals are priceless. I have lost so much money from doing it my way and not the right way. When you know better, you do better. Investing in a professional for small tasks like scheduling, social media, and correspondence to free up time to do other things with my family or work on other projects has also been a worthwhile investment. I will always invest in the best teacher and be the best student if it will make me a good teacher to someone else.

If you lost everything today, what would you do for the next thirty days to generate income?

If I lost everything today, I would take some time to pray for understanding and strategy to reset and restart. I would think about my gifts and how they could generate income without any start-up money. One thing I have is the gift to communicate and inspire. This would allow me to keep my customer base by engaging with them through social media while figuring out my next move. There are multiple ways to reset if you want. If money is needed for what I chose to do, there are a few options. I could:

- Liquidate some designer items that sell well online.
- Borrow from a life insurance policy that has a cash value.
- Apply for a small business loan.
- Get an investor who believes in my vision.

Once I received the start-up money, I would have to evaluate what I have done that would cost me to lose everything so I don't make the same mistake twice. I would think about what I sell the best and the fastest. That would be my starting point. I would start with a low MOQ (minimal order quantity) from my vendors if I planned to continue a product-based business. I would host a BOGO workshop for my Built 2 Build business clients and offer a free fifteen-minute consultation for first-timers. I would stock just enough products to begin to generate an income. I would take a portion of the money and invest it in stocks and/or crypto. I like investing. It's an easy way to generate income without having to do anything.

How can people connect with you?

I can be emailed at info@built2buildnation.com and found on Instagram @Tinabooker_Official.

I'M A STRONG BELIEVER THAT WE ALL HAVE A STORY AND THAT THEY ARE ALL WORTHY OF SHARING.

Camille Campins-Adams

CHAPTER 6

WE ALL HAVE A STORY BY CAMILLE CAMPINS-ADAMS

Hopes. Dreams. Aspirations. We all have them. My middle son has a vivid imagination. He lives for the picturesque realities dreamed up in his head. There's rarely a moment when he's not retelling the stories flashing clearly in the depths of his little five-year-old mind. Rolling on the floor shirtless while wrestling his stuffed alligator, Brooks will grunt, "Mommy, look at this massive gator I caught! It's five hundred pounds, and man, it was a hard one to pin down!" Brooks speaks with a distinct inflection while pantomiming. Everything about this little guy of mine is expressive; so much can be deconstructed from his body language alone. This is standard Brooks. And I see so much of myself in him.

When I was a young girl, I lived in the clouds, your typical dreamer, very much like my little guy. His ability to dream will serve him well as he gets older, and I look forward to seeing where his dreams will one day take him. Dreams can change over time, but it's important to recognize they're limitless. We can and should dream big, because as the famous saying by Norman Vincent Peale goes, "Shoot for the moon. Even if you miss, you'll land among the stars." I've always had lofty dreams, and even though many of them have changed throughout the years, the one that has remained constant is my desire to be an accomplished author.

Right after graduating from high school, a little voice inside me started nudging me toward writing a book. The idea sounded nice, but I knew nothing about the *what, when,* or *how* of becoming an author. This subtle push toward writing would become a much larger thrust once I reached adulthood, but with no real understanding of how the publishing world worked, the goal of publishing a book—let alone multiple books—always felt like a monumental feat; for years, I told myself the odds were against me. Still, I would write in my journal periodically and be in awe of the creative works of those who had reached the pinnacle of success around me.

Despite this being a dream I held, I never really considered it a career path I could follow. Every possible doubt that could creep in about pursuing the life of a writer overtook me. So when I applied to the University of Miami for my undergraduate studies and was told I had to pick a degree, I glazed over English and immediately landed on business. Yes, English was alluring, but what would I ever do with a degree like that? That wasn't a degree that guaranteed any success upon graduating, so I did the most practical and pragmatic thing I could think of: I studied business.

In my junior year of high school, I watched as my older sister competed on the first season of *The Apprentice* with now-former President Donald Trump. Watching her and other successful businessmen and women on television made me realize business would be a smart choice, particularly entrepreneurship. When I chose to study entrepreneurship at age seventeen, I did it partly because I thought it would be one of the easier degrees to graduate with quickly, but I had no idea I would one day be sitting here writing about my life as an entrepreneur. Yet here we are. Life is full of surprises!

It was 2005, right in the middle of the big housing boom, and my sister, who is nearly eight years my senior, was slaying it in real estate; she had just opened her real estate brokerage after coming off *The Apprentice* in sixth place. As I watched her succeed, I figured I could do the same. Katrina was and still is in the top 1 percent of realtors nationwide. She is not your average realtor by any measure, and with that sort of mentor, I told myself to forget about writing and instead take up real estate. The market in 2005 was utterly insane, and the potential to make millions was staring me in the face, making ignoring it financially irresponsible—or so I told myself. Naturally then, I got my real estate license as soon as I could and dove into real estate head-on.

For years, I followed Katrina around. We went to all sorts of fancy events and sold property to the rich and famous. Katrina's roster of clients is something to envy—from pro athletes and musicians to actors and business moguls. Her drive never ceases to amaze me; she started a sports and entertainment division before it was even a thing—and when all the doubters told her she was crazy. Today, there are sports and entertainment divisions in nearly every large brokerage. Although I wasn't pouring into my writing at this time, I was blessed to experience the highs and lows of the industry and watch as my sister blazed trails, all while working next to her. Katrina also has a huge passion for television. During my time working with her, I was featured in an E! segment, filmed various television shows, and flew private. I lived the life that many dream of, but I always knew the time would come for me to move onto other things. In particular, marriage and motherhood.

In spring 2012, I found myself up late one night surfing the internet. I was sitting on a barstool perched up on the kitchen counter of the cozy one-thousand-square-foot cottage my husband David and I were renting in Coconut Grove, Florida. We had just celebrated our first anniversary, and our Labrador mix and three black cats were sleeping close by, always keeping me company in David's absence as he spent months away playing baseball. David and I started dating back in middle school. He proposed to me on our tenth dating anniversary, and we were married less than six months later. Since he was four, David has been clear on his passion. This is not hyperbole; he has had a passion for baseball since he picked up a ball. He knew where he wanted to be when he grew up: a major league baseball field.

I honestly don't remember my exact reasons for being on the computer that night, but I do know it was at that moment I decided I wanted to start writing. Really writing, because even though my dreams of being a published author were deep inside me, my creativity needed to be unleashed. Surprisingly, even to me, my aspirations of being a writer were not evident to those around me. If I'm honest, I never shared that part of myself. I spoke very little of my love for writing, and those closest to me have admitted they had no idea I aspired to write. I'm not sure why I didn't share this about myself; perhaps it was because I didn't see it as clearly then as I do now, or maybe it's because I felt it was a dumb dream to have. Whatever the case, I've now learned that all dreams are valid no matter how outlandish.

It's easy to look back and say I've always appreciated books and the art of writing, but I did nothing to show it. I spent years focused elsewhere, not even finding time to read much, if at all. As I sit back and reflect on why I was so aloof about my writing, it comes down to my never actually taking writing seriously. We live in a world driven by money and power. We need money to survive. It is a necessity; therefore, whatever I was going to achieve in life would have to lead toward prosperity. Truthfully, and quite ignorantly—or maybe that is too harsh and more naive—I never looked at writing as something I could do for a living and make money.

The idea of starting to write for fun—and in particular, to blog about my life as a baseball wife—seemed exciting and easy. I wasn't out to monetize my writing, so it was low pressure and gave me something to do while I traveled with David as he pursued his dreams of reaching the MLB. I honestly didn't even care if anyone read my words. I was writing purely for the sake of writing. Before having this revelation, I quit working in real estate and decided it was time to start anew with my husband. I was tired of spending months apart from him, and I wanted to experience the rush of living a nomadic life while I still could, pre-home and pre-kids. It was clear that the time had come to leave real estate behind and start fresh. So with my little online blog and our three animals, I left Miami behind and started traveling with David.

A year after I started documenting my life as a baseball wife, which eventually did gain traction and was picked up by MLBlogs.com, David and I found ourselves living in a small fully furnished rental in Tampa for spring training. David had a real shot of making the team, and we were looking forward to what the future held. To make things even more exciting, I soon found out I was pregnant with our first child.

That spring was full of highs and lows. First, David sustained a back injury that cost him his job. Right after I told him we were expecting, the Yankees notified him they needed to make space on their roster, and since he was, for all intents and purposes, dead weight at the time, he was the one to go. He never had the chance to play that spring due to his back, and his future in baseball went from bright to dim in a flash. Although the situation resolved itself in our favor rather quickly and ended up being a blessing, it left us shaken. Then several days later, I received a phone call from my sister that the reality show she had been pitching for over a year had been greenlighted and we would start filming very soon. So much was happening all at once, and I struggled to share any of it through my writing.

My story was in me. It wanted and needed to be shared, but so many things continued to stop me. The overwhelm. The fear of judgment. The worries that I would offend someone. Worst of all, the debilitating thoughts kept creeping in: *Who am I to share my story? Who cares what I have to say? David isn't even a big leaguer. Our story isn't important. Who cares about life in the minor leagues? I'm just the wife; he's the star. So just shut up and stop writing. You are irrelevant.* I felt and thought all of it, and as a result, my writing dried up.

After spring training, instead of moving up with David to Pennsylvania where the Yankees' Triple-A team played, I went back to Miami to film *Hot Listings Miami*. The show featured me as a realtor working with my sister, but the truth was, I had already moved on from that and I was resentful that I couldn't spend the beginning of the season with David instead. I know it sounds crazy, but I never wanted to be on television; I did it as a way to support my sister in her dreams. Looking back, I wish I would've seized the moment instead of being hyper-focused on the anger I held toward my sister for holding me back from what I wanted at the time: to be traveling with David.

Between 2008 and 2013, I found myself surrounded by very wealthy, successful people, but I never felt like the standout, and you can forget about feeling successful. My sister had this incredible career, was friends with many celebrities, and was a recognized face by many. And my husband, who did make his major league debut right in the middle of my filming *Hot Listings Miami*, became famous among baseball fans quite literally overnight. He was trending on Twitter the day of his debut and was doing back-to-back interviews for several weeks. Sandwiched between these extremes, I was playing witness to the incredible success of two people I loved and figured my role was merely to support them. Given the circumstances and my introverted tendencies, I was fine being the person behind-the-scenes. However, watching their lives unfold as they reached great heights made me even more insecure about sharing my story. David and Katrina are the type of people publishers want knocking at their door with a book idea, but what about me?

Did my story still matter?

I officially stopped blogging about my life as a baseball wife when David made his big league debut. It was incredibly hard for me to talk about any blessings that were coming our way, especially when I had spent a year writing about how hard it was to be in the minor leagues, even as a high-ranking prospect. I wrote many blog posts about the challenges that come from living and pursuing "the dream," and now I felt incapable of sharing how our story had improved. Even though David's major league career was riddled with injuries and trials, and it didn't last nearly as long as we'd hoped, I struggled to share about it. Then once we welcomed our first baby, Jethro, finding time to write felt impossible.

Despite not writing, my dreams of being published were still ever present. Deep in my bones, I felt this calling to share *my* story, whatever that looked like.

A few years later, in 2016, David retired from playing baseball and transitioned into coaching. At this point, we had two boys (we welcomed Brooks in 2015), ages one and three. As his playing career came to an end, David decided to finish his undergraduate degree. He was drafted by the Yankees his third year at the University of Virginia, so he had about a year of schooling left to finish. Motivated by my husband's drive to go back and finish his degree, I decided to continue my education in the form of a master's degree.

At first, I had no idea what type of degree I wanted to pursue, but I knew I wanted it to be related to writing. It may have taken me years, but I finally began to acknowledge that the writing world was where I needed to be. In my search for options, I discovered the MFA and MA in creative writing. I had no idea there was such a thing as getting a master's degree in creative writing, but it fit all the criteria I was looking for in a program. Very quickly, I got my butt in gear and started applying to low-residency programs that would provide the flexibility I needed to plow through my degree while raising two preschool children.

Studying creative writing is the greatest gift I have given myself, outside of my children, of course. Having children is a calling and an assignment most of us are given in our lifetime, but studying writing is purely for me. Getting an advanced degree in creative writing allowed me to dedicate time to the craft, hone my skills as a writer, and, arguably most important of all, support other writers.

Every preconceived notion I held of what it meant to be a writer was turned on its head during my time in school. When writing is something you aspire to do, it should never feel like a burden, yet so many of us feel an enormous weight on our shoulders to produce works of art that speak to the masses. While in school, I realized our work will never appeal to the majority of the world, and still, that is almost entirely the point. I have learned to accept that the stories many of us have to share will only resonate with a fraction of the readers that populate this earth. Still, that doesn't make them any less worthy of telling.

There are billions of people in the world. So even though your story will not speak to everyone, it will speak to someone, and that leaves you with an enormous responsibility to share it. Telling your unique story can impact many lives, even when you doubt it can. Additionally, I often argue that writing or publishing a book for a larger audience doesn't have to be your end goal. Many people document their stories for their families or to work through trauma. Writing can be an incredibly cathartic process, and you don't have to consider yourself a skilled writer to start putting pen to paper. Writing can be healing, and I highly encourage it as a practice that everyone can do.

Since my personal goal has always been to publish a book, I went into grad school with the goal of writing a memoir. I graduated with a good chunk of my memoir written in the form of my thesis and was on a mission to get my book done, my proposal written, and my agent queries submitted. I spent months tweaking and preparing a proposal and writing agent queries, but then I stopped. I was frozen because I realized my memoir wasn't and still isn't quite ready for publication. My memoir is a special project of mine and one I am in no rush to publish. Although I would love to get it out into the world one day, I'll be okay if that never comes to fruition because I know I am leaving my family many pages of stories they can pass down for generations. That alone makes the pages I have saved worth something.

In using my newly honed skills, I began working as a freelance writer. I've spent years writing blogs, emails, press releases, website copy, and so much more for businesses. I have been blessed to monetize my writing, but my passion is still with stories, especially books. Although I have always loved reading, school taught me how critical being well-read is. Reading makes you a better writer, and we should be reading even more than we are writing. Each semester in grad school, we were required to read seven books and write an extensive analysis of them. We were expected to read books with a critical eye to understand better what makes a compelling book. I invested hundreds of hours analyzing the works of other writers and trying to understand the craft better.

While growing my writing business, I had clients approach me about helping them write books. I was fascinated by the idea and started looking into getting certified as a book coach. Today, I continue to write for a living, but what's most gratifying is helping other writers pen and share their own stories. I'm a strong believer that we all have a story and that they are all worthy of sharing. So even when you feel like your story doesn't matter, it does.

What is your *why* or purpose for your business?

My *why*, first and foremost, is my family. Yes, I want to do something every day that fuels my soul, but my family is my greatest blessing. I work so I can provide a better future for us. So that I can live free of mom guilt and be present when it matters most. With three young kids, it's important for me to be home with them, especially with the demands that baseball places on our family.

David is often traveling or at the field fourteen to sixteen hours a day. However, being the backbone of my family is the most vital job I have, and being a writer and book coach allows me the freedom to work from anywhere while still being present for my children. Even better, I get to do what I love: read and write all day long.

Additionally, I know how it feels to have a story inside of you. To feel like you can't rest until you release it. I know every person has a story, and I want to help people get their books out into the world. Very few things excite me as good books do, and I'm privileged to help others tell their stories.

What is one of your greatest failures that ultimately led to success?

I honestly don't see failures in life. What I see are opportunities for growth—learning experiences and opportunities to get to know yourself better and what matters to you. For me, one of the things I continued to try throughout the years was real estate. Even when I walked away from it, I tried coming back, yet every time I have done a deal, I have been left stressed, bitter, and extremely frustrated. There are so many reasons why this is, but mostly it has to do with expectations. I am really bad about setting boundaries. Boundaries are something we need to set with all clients, in real estate and in book coaching. Recognizing I am an over-giver has helped me make shifts in my business and learn how important boundaries are.

In addition to that, I am not passionate about real estate. So it's no wonder when a client calls me while I'm at the movies with my family, I get upset and want to cry. Trying to do something that does not align with my values for the sake of money has never ended well. Through this, I've learned that I need to stick with what lights me up. Yes, I walked away from writing time and time again, but I kept coming back, because trying other things validated even further how much I truly love the world of books and writing.

What is your biggest day-to-day struggle in running your business?

Time. I still struggle with juggling all the things because I like to move fast. I have very few hours each day to get work done because of the kids, so I honestly only work three hours a day, max. I would love to work more, simply because I love it, but I have made it a priority to be present when I'm with my children; they are young, and these times are fleeting. I know I will have time for work later, but they will grow up and move on before I know it. For these reasons, I have had to accept that sometimes growth comes in the form of incremental action. Rome wasn't built in a day, so I have to give myself the grace to take my time without putting immense pressure on myself.

What is the most worthwhile investment you have made for your business?

The most valuable investment you can ever make in your business and otherwise is in yourself. Everything in your life can go up in flames, but you will come out stronger if you are equipped with knowledge and skills. So my answer is simple: myself.

If you lost everything today, what would you do for the next thirty days to generate income?

Find a single, marketable skill I know I am good at and offer it as a service. In my case, it's writing. I believe that our network is powerful and that relationships matter. Therefore, I would reach out to five people a day and let them know what I do. I would not try to push any of my services on them, but rather genuinely connect and make them aware of my current offers and what I am doing in my business. I would also make sure they know I would be grateful for referrals. You would be surprised how quickly you can fill your roster of clients by simply reaching out to your sphere of influence.

How can people connect with you?

I can be found at CampinsAdams.com.

BEING THAT PERSON OTHERS LOOK UP TO AND THINK "IF SHE CAN DO IT, SO CAN I" IS THE MOST REWARDING FEELING.

Brianna Coon

CHAPTER 7

A MEANS OF SURVIVAL BY BRIANNA COON

Starting my business was a means of survival for me. I don't just mean financial and having a steady paycheck. I had spent all my "career-forming" years as an employee. I was bouncing from industry to industry because I wasn't sure what I wanted to do. From an incredibly young age, I always identified with growing up and being a veterinarian, as I loved all animals. I was the kind of girl who brought home wounded animals, nursed them back to health, and then released them back to Mother Nature. However, as I moved through the education system, I quickly realized that academics were not my strong suit. After having some difficult conversations with my parents, school advisors, and other mentors in my life, I knew this wasn't going to be the path for me anymore.

As a young woman graduating from high school having "lost" a piece of who I thought I was destined to be, I knew I had my work cut out for me. I ended up taking an online program to get my Animal Sciences Certification while working up to five jobs at one time because I wanted to dip my toes in every industry to see where I fit in. I was looking for that sense of belonging from a job. From hospitality, retail, and nonprofit organizations to even a doggy daycare! But again, nothing quite fit that missing puzzle piece I had in my life.

I hit a point where everything came to a halt when I got fired for the first time. I was a part-time receptionist at a spa, and I was going above and beyond (in my eyes), looking for different ideas to improve the business and the overall customer experience and company visibility. I was so ashamed when my boss sat me down and told me that I wasn't a good fit because I was going outside the scope of the role and she wanted someone who would punch in and punch out.

From there, I had a moment of realization that I wanted to find a "big girl" job. A role in which I could grow within a company and learn different things, where my motivation and determination would be recognized and appreciated. I beefed up my résumé and was on the look again for a job. That's when I came into the real estate industry. I started with a new home builder at the very bottom of the food chain. When I look back at it, the best way I can describe it is like the movie *The Devil Wears Prada*. For lack of a better word, I was my boss's "bitch." I put up with many things I shouldn't have, but I didn't know any better. I was learning so much about sales, marketing, construction, and how the industry worked that I let all of those other things slide.

Meanwhile, in my personal life, I was allowing for more damaging and dangerous behavior to slide as well. At age twenty, I had found myself deep in a mentally, financially, and physically abusive relationship. Without going into all the details, I allowed him to chip away at me piece by piece—my self-worth, confidence, and who I truly was until I was barely recognizable to my friends, family, and myself. I allowed people to step all over me because I didn't think I was valuable enough to be treated as an asset in a personal dynamic and a professional one. Once I got out of the personal abusive relationship and started rebuilding myself, I recognized those red flags in my work relationships. I requested for changes to be made, and then my career began to soar. I found a man who truly accepted me for who I was, cheered me on, and supported me with whatever challenge I wanted to take. I was *finally* getting the recognition for the talents I always knew I had!

I became a key member of the marketing and sales department. I became the highest-paid senior sales associate the company had, and they still use the social media strategies I created and piloted.

But then I hit another glass ceiling.

Instead of allowing this to hold me back, I made another shift in my career path. I loved real estate and still do, but I decided to move into commercial. I worked with a well-known team in my city as their team coordinator, and I assisted with all kinds of things I loved.

Then in December 2019, those dreaded words coursed through my ears again: "It's just not a good fit . . ."

Saying I was devastated was an understatement. At age twenty-four, I had been fired from an industry that I was excelling at. I felt rejected and deflated. I had my pity party for a few days, and then as my grandfather would say, I pulled up my bootstraps and put my big-girl pants back on and was on the search again. But I was going to do it differently this time. I was not going to allow myself to settle and take the first thing that came my way. I wanted the control and the respect I deserved. Going on job interviews with a different mindset opened my eyes to what I wanted and that I could say no. The interview that forever changed my life was for a role similar to what I had as a team coordinator but for a residential realtor and his team. He wanted me to work for him as a subcontractor.

Once I looked into what that meant and what the role was that he described, it sparked a light-bulb moment for me. I had all these skills that I had learned from all the different industries I had worked in, and I could help so many business owners without having to be tied to just one company. This is how Limitless Impact Virtual Management was born!

As a virtual business consultant and social media strategist, I provide business owners with impactful services to make their work life more enjoyable. I assist them with all aspects of their day-to-day operations and build a social media and marketing strategy specifically tailored to their goals. Many business owners who are starting or are in the middle of a growth period when they are not ready to hire a full-time employee but still need the help with the overwhelming tasks lean on me to continue to push their businesses further. I have grown my business from just me to five other subcontractors under me, with over forty clients around North America while earning five-figure months in just eighteen months.

What is your *why* or purpose for your business?

Being in business for myself and being a young entrepreneur gave me the sense of control and purpose I was looking for in my life. When it comes to explaining my *why* or the purpose of my business, it is so much more than that. Yes, I went into business to make money, but I also was looking for a sense of fulfillment and self-recognition that I was longing for. I love being able to help fellow entrepreneurs worldwide grow their businesses, reach their goals, and be a part of their team and their success. This is what gets me out of bed in the morning and drives me to work those extra hours because I know I'm achieving my *dream* and helping others achieve theirs.

Being that person others look up to and think "If she can do it, so can I" is the most rewarding feeling. I'm educating other young entrepreneurs on creating a future for themselves without having to work for a company that views them as a number or as replaceable. They can ask me those questions they think are "stupid," knowing that I won't judge them. When it comes down to the core values of my business, I am here to educate and support, to be the cheerleader, the shoulder to cry on, and to help my client's businesses exceed what they think it's capable of.

What are the biggest mistakes you see new entrepreneurs making?

When I started my business in December 2019, I had no expectations of how it would perform. I knew I wanted to be the one in control, make the rules, and decide what would happen. I reached out to the people in my network who I knew needed support but weren't quite at the point where they needed a full-time or even a part-time employee but needed someone to help take some tasks off their plates.

Once I started getting positive feedback, and the word began to spread about my business, I took on clients left and right. I sold every hour of my day to help my clients. I worked fourteen-to-eighteen-hour days trying to keep up with the work coming in. Don't get me wrong, I loved the work because I was passionate about what I was doing, but I noticed it was starting to take a toll on my personal life and health.

I took on clients for whom I had those little red flags pop up in our initial conversations, but I ignored them. I was allowing my clients to tiptoe over my boundaries and not correcting them when they did. This is such a common mistake new business owners make because they want to keep up with the momentum and not say no. The biggest mistake I see fellow entrepreneurs making, myself included, is not allowing themselves to say no to new work or clients who are disrespecting their boundaries. Once you allow these clients or any other people involved with your business to treat you like this, it's hard to correct it later down the line. Always make sure to stay true to your rules/policies/boundaries, as this can be harmful to yourself and your business in the future if you don't.

Which activities do you perform that generate the majority of your revenue?

Every entrepreneur has different strategies they rely on when sales are low to generate more revenue for themselves and their businesses. I always stay on top of my business's revenue, so when I notice that a month is a little slower than normal, I turn to the things that work for my business to create more cash flow, such as:

- Outreach
  - I reach out to podcasts, radio shows, and any sort of media to see if I can secure a spot as a guest to increase my visibility and exposure to new clients.
- Social media
  - I pick up my social media game! I reach out to other people in my industry to see if we can do some sort of partnership or collaboration that would benefit us and create extra revenue.
- Referrals
  - I talk with my current clients, friends, and family to see if anyone in their network is looking for someone like me to help them with their business.
- Business networking groups
  - I'm part of a Business Network International (BNI) chapter in my city. I highly recommend any entrepreneur new in the game or a seasoned vet to join and regularly attend a business networking group, as I have gained so much from being a member. Not only do I gain more clients, but I learn something new from every meeting.

What is your biggest day-to-day struggle in running your business?

I have struggled with imposter syndrome on and off for the last eighteen months. I started my business in January 2020 (just before shit hit the fan), and I knew that I was strong, intelligent, brave, and capable enough to handle everything that would be thrown my way the first year of running my business, but what I wasn't prepared for was imposter syndrome.

I have friends, family, clients, and strangers who tell me all the time how amazing I am at what I do and how creative and smart my business is (and I don't say this to brag), but when I hear those words for some reason, my brain turns into mush. I don't know how to comprehend and truly receive the kind words they're saying. I know I'm not the only business owner or young entrepreneur who battles this feeling.

There are so many blogs and other influencers that post tips and tricks about tackling this feeling. No one talks about taking a moment and truly sitting with the feeling and appreciating what you are experiencing in that moment! When I have those moments, I sit there, reflect, and remind myself why I am where I am and how I got there. For example:

- I worked my ass off to grow my business to a team of five, to make a consistent five figures each month, and to work with over forty clients across North America.
- I put myself out there by reaching out to podcast creators and other business owners to potentially partner with, expecting to be told no but being told yes.
- I was nominated for the 29th Annual RBC Canadian Women Entrepreneur Awards presented by Women of Influence under the category of "Ones to Watch."
- I've been featured on multiple podcast interviews and a monthly radio show and have been a guest speaker at networking events.

It's *okay* to sit in this feeling and give yourself the time to truly feel like an imposter, but remember you are the badass business owner who got yourself where you are today. You are worthy of all the success coming your way! Believe in that!

What have you found helps with blending your personal and professional life?

This is something that I struggle with. Being a virtual-based business and working from home, work is always accessible to me. Along with setting boundaries with your clients and other people involved in your business, you must set boundaries between yourself and your work. There are countless books, blogs, and articles that talk about this because it's an area where entrepreneurs do struggle.

The practice that has helped me create a healthier work-life balance is time blocking and creating hard limits of how much I will work per day and week. A hard limit for me is that I will not work on the weekends. Instead, I will use that time to unplug, spend time with my loved ones, and do the things I love to help me unwind and relax. Sunday nights, I review my upcoming week and make a list of tasks from high to low priority.

With the help of my team of subcontractors, I can lean on them when there are many different things my clients need to get accomplished within a specific time frame. By time blocking my schedule, I can give myself the breaks my body and mind need to function to be at the top of my game. I only schedule a certain number of meetings per day and stagger them with client work so I maintain a steady pace and avoid feeling overwhelmed. I highly recommend incorporating this strategy into your day-to-day work life to improve your productivity and maintain a healthy work-life balance!

What self-care, routines, and habits do you have to maintain good health?

When running a business, there can be a lot of pressure hanging over your head. It's crucial to make yourself a priority amid the responsibility carried on your shoulders. To take care of my physical body, I make sure to schedule regular appointments with my chiropractor and massage therapist. I take walks around my neighborhood during the day to step away from the computer and unplug for a bit to clear my head.

Taking care of your mental health is crucial. If you're not in a good mindset, your clients and your business will notice. Allowing yourself to find a practice that works for you to process your emotions and thoughts is important. I use a daily journal app on my phone to write out what I am grateful for and how I feel. If I'm having a bad day, I write it out to process and get to the root cause. I lean on my family, boyfriend, and friends for support when I have those moments to vent and let it out so I'm not holding on to whatever is bothering me.

Having a hobby outside of your business is a way to get involved with other activities to promote a healthy work-life balance. I love plants, gardening, and anything that has to do with being outdoors. I can express my creativity by playing with different types of flowers and arrangements in the garden and honoring the nurturing side of me by taking care of my plants. Finding things that bring joy outside of business is the best way to take care of and honor yourself!

What is the most worthwhile investment you have made for your business?

By far, the most worthwhile investment was investing in myself and always staying up-to-date on current trends by enrolling in master classes and courses taught by the industry's top influencers. I take care of myself by practicing self-care, working on my mental and physical health, and taking breaks/time off to prevent burnout. My clients rely on me to be at my best, so it's imperative that I invest in myself. No matter what industry your business is in, this should be a priority. You are no help to your paying clients when you are in a burnout haze. Invest in the things that make you happy.

If you lost everything today, what would you do for the next thirty days to generate income?

Our future is unknown. We can prepare for disasters and the "what if" situations all we want, but we don't know how we will react and overcome those events until they happen. If I were to lose everything, I would take a step back. I would elevate what caused this to happen and how I could have prevented it, and then I'd set myself up so it doesn't happen again. Based on the answers to these reflection questions, I would return to the basics. Reinvent my business plan, recreate my marketing plan/strategy, and increase my visibility of who I am, my business, and why I am doing what I do. I would reach out to others in my industry to see if there is an opportunity for a working partnership to tap into their network. With the struggle of 2020, I understand many businesses have had to close their doors or start from square one, but it comes down to one thing: if you love what you do and believe that you can be successful, the universe will provide you a way to get back on track.

How can people connect with you?

I can be found at limitlessimpact.ca and on Instagram @limitlessimpact.

MY PURPOSE IS TO EMPOWER WOMEN TO LOVE THEMSELVES AS THEY ARE AND UPLIFT THEM TO BELIEVE THEY BELONG NO MATTER WHO THEY ARE AND WHAT THEY LOOK LIKE.

Aranzasu De La O

CHAPTER 8

EMPOWERMENT COMES FROM WITHIN BY ARANZASU DE LA O

When I was a little girl, I felt like the slowest, the least intelligent, and the most behind of all my peers. I felt too dark to be pretty. I felt scared to speak up and I was insecure. Someone once told me that I had to work extra hard since my parents were Mexican immigrants, which deeply affected my psyche.

One of the reasons I started my wellness coaching business was to empower as many women as possible to prioritize inner peace and love themselves more.

I spent most of my life feeling anxious and worried that I'd never make it, which brought me so much fear and chronic anxiety. While I understand that I had mountains to climb to "catch up" to other peers, believing I was less than was painful and drove me to do many things out of fear of not being worthy enough.

Yet I see my story as an advantage. Feeling like the underdog built up my fire and discipline. To this day, I am proud of my work ethic in many areas of my life and how far I've come. My story is similar to many children of immigrants and Latinas who grew up in Los Angeles in the '90s. Many of us are still making sense of who we are and are slowly but surely building up our self-esteem. The impact of the attacks we felt on our family, culture, and background shook up our confidence. We survived anti-immigrant California state policies that shattered our spirit, but this didn't break us. I certainly didn't let this stifle my motivation.

My business ensures that these women believe in themselves and, most importantly, understand their magnificence for being who they are. I make sure my services transform women from the inside out to be the change they wish to see in the world.

I grew up in a low-income community of Santa Monica referred to as the "Pico Neighborhood," and I was constantly worried my family and I would be evicted from our apartment. I was very determined to succeed. The internal and external pressure to uplift my family, culture, and neighborhood drove me, but I realize now that it created a lot of anxiety. My passion for dance, fitness, and nutrition helped me cope, but I still couldn't shake the fear that I needed to work hard nonstop.

The pressure started when I was nine years old. By that time, I didn't know how to play spontaneously anymore. I felt that if I stopped doing anything productive, I would get behind and never reach my dream of going to college. As a child, I trained hard for dance competitions, volunteered, took on extra Saturday classes at the local community college, and attended many college and scholarship workshops. I maintained a 4.0 GPA through most of middle school and high school. I knew I needed to cover all my bases to make it out of the Pico Neighborhood and help my family succeed.

My efforts led me to the University of Southern California, Washington, DC Harvard University, and Wall Street. In addition, I lived and studied abroad in Italy, worked in Brazil, and most recently lived in Guatemala.

The need to "catch up," being scared of the police, and the hateful rhetoric I experienced as a child created detrimental emotional distress for me. I also understand that not everyone who experienced something similar was able to come out of that. It's a grave mental health issue that is shared in communities with similar demographics.

For a long time, I was haunted by my aunt's voice as she wailed over my cousin's casket. Eddie was killed by a single gunshot that hit his back and penetrated his heart. Eddie's last words were "My mom . . ." and his eyes shut forever. He fell by a tree in front of the theater where I often performed. For a long time, especially throughout my time at Harvard, I panicked every time I got a phone call from my mother. I was afraid that something horrible had happened to my brothers.

Over the years, I've created meticulous wellness practices and morning rituals that allow women like me to ease trauma and to thrive and heal from the inside out. My hope is that other women and little girls of color who suffer from chronic stress and worry of survival can truly believe they will make it. I want them to understand that we are worthy and whole just for being who we are.

What is your *why* or purpose for your business?

A *big* source of inspiration is driven by my immediate family and my Mexican heritage. When I think of my parents and siblings, I am filled with pride, love, and purpose. When I hear the Mexican guitar or harps or the voice of Lila Downs, I feel harmony in my heart and sometimes cry. (Look up the soundtrack from *Frida,* the film, and you'll understand why.) I am intensely connected to my Latino culture, and my mission is to elevate the voices of women and communities that have felt disempowered and marginalized.

My purpose is to empower women to love themselves as they are and uplift them to believe they belong no matter who they are and what they look like. I want to make sure every woman of color who ever felt less than or anxious or who felt stuck in a pit can come out of the darkness. My goal is for these women to give themselves permission to experience more play and joy and to get stronger from the inside out.

Accepting myself as I am didn't come easy. Growing up as a brown Mexican-American girl in LA in the '90s brought a whirlwind of identity issues and conflicting emotions. Feeling comfortable in my skin and loving myself has been a painful, evolving process. I spent my life believing I was less than and never Mexican or American enough. My name and my physical attributes are ambiguous. Mexicans are typically confused by my Basque name and how I look. Americans don't even know where to get started.

Since I was a child, I've attempted to understand my identity. As soon as I could get a passport, I took trips to Mexico by myself to connect with two of the women who raised my mother (my great aunts). I told my mother I didn't want help figuring out how to get around to visit family in Mexico. I wanted to navigate my journey by myself.

I put a lot of planning and effort into getting to know my extended family in Mexico, but now I realize I sometimes felt sad and lonely in the process. I realized my family's cultural traditions in the US would slowly deteriorate over time from the grind and a lifetime of manual labor, and we'd likely spend most of our lives trading health and sanity for the so-called American Dream. This brought me deep despair.

But I put a stake in the ground. I resolved that no person or idea would determine how I wanted to live my life, how I felt about myself, and how I identified. As a result, I no longer crave the need to find my identity. Every day I work on my scarcity and mental roadblocks in regard to lack of success.

What I crave the most is having the best health, living my life with meaning, and defining success on my terms, because this brings me the most peace and helps me move forward. I spend my energy growing my business, learning new skills, making plant-based meals that fuel me, moving my body, and retesting self-care practices that elevate my whole wellness, especially my mental and emotional health.

I am proud of my efforts to find myself and my identity, but it was so exhausting. I am now more comfortable with my identity, whatever it may be, as I'm sure it will evolve and change. I am particularly grateful that I found my grandfather in Tequila, Jalisco, where my mother was born.

I took a trip to Tequila once, and when I arrived at the main plaza, I asked an older gentleman if they'd heard of "Quirios," which was my grandfather's nickname. I'd never met my grandfather and he didn't raise my mother, but I found him on this special trip. When I first caught a glimpse of my grandfather at his home, he was playing the guitar in his bedroom. He came out to greet me with joy and offered me a shot of Tequila. I couldn't stop smiling, and he wouldn't stop sharing how much he loved my grandmother and my mother. Through this experience, I reconnected my mother with her sisters. I will always cherish this memory.

My connection with my culture has been a big part of my life and the need to balance my mental and emotional health. Both drive the mission and vision of my business. For example, for a long time, I couldn't sit still for too long or even watch a movie without feeling anxious or falling asleep. But when I met my sweet twelve-year-old Yorkie, Chulo, it became easier for me to relax.

Chulo moved so slowly through the block (except if he smelled french fries) that I had no choice but to walk at his pace. I practiced being fully present with him at every moment, and he brought me so much happiness. Chulo cracked my heart open. He was everything I needed to understand the fullness of my love, loss, and the distress of my anxiety. I helped Chulo cross the rainbow when he was fifteen and a half, and it was the most excruciating, painful act of love I have ever experienced. My heart broke when Chulo parted, and I also got COVID-19 right after he transitioned.

During my stint with COVID, I was tormented with horrible symptoms, including nightmares and panic attacks. I felt more alone and isolated than I'd ever felt in my life. I didn't have anyone close to support me, so I leaned on my wellness rituals to comfort and help me cope. I lost weight. I was sad. And I didn't know I needed support to grieve the loss of Chulo fully. I may have been at the lowest point of my life.

This experience led me to think even deeper about my purpose, my life, and my business. I leaned on my spiritual, food, and body rituals like never before, which helped me crawl out of suffering relatively quickly. I remember thinking that if I came out of this dark moment alive, I would leave for Guatemala for a long time and spend an indefinite amount of time in Lago de Atitlán (Lake Atitlan).

I envisioned myself climbing Mayan mountains and volcanoes around the lake, meditating to my favorite Buddhist chants, drinking Mayan cacao, eating good food, and connecting with the Mayan community. I badly wanted to live in Guatemala to connect with my true essence and ancestors and heal from the inside out. I was also very curious about Mayan cacao, as it is often referred to as "heart medicine." It was this vision that gave me a lot of hope.

I can confidently tell you that the only way I regained my whole wellness in a very healthy way was through countless hours of meditation, breathwork, body movement, myofascial release, and tapping therapy (EFT: emotional freedom technique). I also raised the bar in my plant-based nutrition and refined my morning rituals. It sounds like a lot, but I just did some things every morning consistently. I regained my physical strength first with light walks and strength training (I used heavy rocks that I picked up around the lake) and incorporated steep stairs and hikes. I recovered my energy through mental, emotional, and physical training practices that will serve me well for the rest of my life.

I got more comfortable doing nothing, being by myself, and connecting with my wholeness during this time of travel alone. It was an intense time, as I spent many nights in the dark, no electricity, dead devices, and candles due to harsh rainy conditions.

All I could hear sometimes was my breath muted by thunderstorms and lightning. I also got water poisoning often, which was hard on my body. Some days, I had no choice but to take naps and be out for a while to regain my energy.

There was something so profound about these moments. They deepened my journey into self-love and wholeness, and I connected deeper with my mission and purpose.

What are the biggest mistakes you see new entrepreneurs making?

Disconnecting with our:

1. why,
2. health, and
3. grit.

I know very well what it's like to get lost in the academic, corporate, and entrepreneurship ladders. Like anyone else, most entrepreneurs forget about their *why* and get lost in the grind. The moment I connect with my *why* and my health, I feel inspired and motivated.

It's easy to get disconnected from our purpose with so many distractions. Connecting to our *why* and our whole wellness every day is pivotal to strengthening our grit muscles. We also need to make sure we're not putting our business before our health, which is easy to do. When we lose track of our physical and emotional health, we lose clarity and can get moody.

I often think about the economics concept known as "diminishing marginal returns" in terms of business and health. In other words, production starts to become less efficient (business and health) when increasing one unit of production (more work). While we may perceive that more input from work is better, our business performance may decrease in the long run if we're not taking care of our mind, body, and mental and emotional well-being.

Being an entrepreneur is just like our whole wellness journey. Entrepreneurship is about managing our energy and being mindfully consistent so we don't burn out. It's the same thing with our wellness and what I teach. Quick fixes, diets, and overnight successes are not part of my philosophy. Consistent practices that last a lifetime and getting comfortable with delayed gratification are part of my mindset in health and business. We must trust the learning process and have courage and faith in our ability to persevere. It's also important to keep in mind that the outcome does not determine our worth or success.

What is one of your greatest failures that ultimately led to success?

My greatest failures were due to my lack of confidence, comparing myself with the apparent "success" of others, and attaching success to external factors and accomplishments. I have slowly but surely gotten out of my own way by focusing on my unique mission and purpose. When I do that, I emerge less fearful than the previous day.

My internal battles stifle my confidence, creativity, and inner peace all the time. The difference now is that I am very aware of them, so instead of seeing my disharmony as failures and roadblocks, I see them as an opportunity to do something different. There's always an opportunity to strengthen our emotional, mental, and physical prowess. I embrace my challenges. I see myself in a battleground sometimes. The more I crawl out of this battleground (i.e., my limiting beliefs and negative thoughts), the stronger I feel, which ignites my fire. Being gentle and kind to myself first is how I turn my failures into action.

What hard lessons have you learned that could have been avoided?

It all comes back to mindset and confidence. I failed to believe in myself. I failed to connect with my story and use it as an inner source of strength.

It's easy to quickly avoid hard feelings that come from challenging moments. But if we look at our challenges straight in the eye, we can use them to understand what they're teaching us and use our lessons to empower other people. We often separate ourselves. We judge ourselves and others and compare each other. This stifles our creativity and growth. This is also a big reason I believe there's so much conflict and hate in the world. This is something I want to change. I want the women I serve to feel great so that together we can be the change I wish to see in the world.

Awareness of our inner-growth process allows us to see how every lesson, event, or person brings us closer to our enlightenment, wholeness, and zone of genius. This is the place where we can better serve the world.

What is your biggest day-to-day struggle in running your business?

In the beginning, I found it difficult to stop working at all hours of the day. This heightened my anxiety and created tension in my relationships. I was pushing and trying too hard instead of taking action with ease, faith, and inspiration. I was determined to do all the things to succeed.

As an entrepreneur, the fears and anxiety I had as a child creep up every day and I constantly doubt myself. But I can see how I also get more and more comfortable with thinking out of the box and sitting in uncertainty. In the beginning, I felt like I needed to catch up all the time. Now I remind myself that I get to do this, and it's a huge privilege and honor to start and grow a business. I focus on a few things, and I'm less hard on myself.

I know for sure that entrepreneurship is just like my whole wellness journey: for a lifetime. I learn as quickly as I can, test, and see how it lands. It's the same concept in our health and fitness. I am constantly learning new technology in my business, figuring out passive profit strategies, converting new clients, and providing the best service. In my health, I am continually assessing and paying attention to my energy and mood. In my business and health, I do my best to celebrate all of my wins, no matter how small they are.

Once I grow my team, I will be able to do things faster and scale my business, but I know that I will always find a way as long as I don't quit. I maintain a schedule and have hard deadlines for myself, but I also prioritize my self-care, whole wellness, and family time. I prefer to focus on quality and getting my mindset right.

When we lose sight of our *whys* and core values, our struggles are magnified. That's why I'm more connected with my *why* now than ever before, and one of my core values is my health and family. I make sure my values are at the center of my activities because family and health are my purpose and inspiration.

What have you found helps with blending your personal and professional life?

My wellness rituals empower my personal and professional life. They help me feel better and keep me calm during challenging times. Making sure my mental state is healthy allows my personal and professional life to be in harmony, which is exactly what I need to grow my business and be the change I wish to see in the world. My wellness rituals (like breathwork and meditation) bring me so much self-awareness. And self-awareness is the key to figuring out where we need to shift and pivot both personally and professionally.

What self-care, routines, and habits do you have to maintain good health?

I love waking up to take care of my mind, body, and soul, and it flows so nicely with wellness rituals and ceremonies I've created. I make sure I wake up every morning with ease. If I'm quick to be in my head, I play healing music on my Insight Timer app. I take deep breaths if any anxiety or worry creeps in. I don't take caffeine to pump me up.

I prepare for the day with soft music and make lukewarm lemon water that I take with a probiotic. I love to have alone time in the morning, and then I make sure I get some morning sunshine if I can. If I can meditate and get sunshine together, then I do this at the same time. I typically meditate for ten to twenty minutes a day.

I hydrate a lot in the mornings and throughout the day. I drink Kangen water (alkaline water), which is rich in minerals, has anti-aging properties, is purged of impurities, and greatly supports skin health and immunity. I enjoy moving my body in the morning, and it usually happens on an empty stomach, but if you find that you need more energy before working out, eating or drinking something before a workout is fine. The best thing we can do is master our energy and figure out what best nourishes us. We are the best students of our bodies.

Most of the time, I have a green smoothie with 85 percent greens and 15 percent fruits, followed by oatmeal after I work out. If I work out later in the day, I monitor my energy levels and make sure I'm not running on low fuel. So if I work out later in the day, by then, I would have already had my greens smoothies, some oatmeal, or a protein smoothie. It's important to gauge your energy.

Some days before or after my green smoothie, I'll have Mayan cacao. I learned about the great benefits of cacao in Guatemala. I use it as a spiritual practice to connect with myself and my culture, but I also use it for health benefits. Cacao is the superfood of all superfoods. It has one of the highest sources of magnesium in nature and it's full of antioxidants, calcium, zinc, copper, and selenium. It's a natural mood elevator.

To holistically connect my wellness practice, I allow my body to have the best sleep possible, and I don't eat for at least fourteen to sixteen hours after my last meal. I naturally practice fasting during this time. I don't get hungry immediately after waking up. I have trained my body over the years to drink water in the mornings before eating anything.

Hydration and constant detoxification are very important. My body doesn't wake up hungry. It wakes up thirsty. I constantly detoxify in the mornings and throughout the day with Kangen water. I have paid very close attention to my body's needs over the years and learned that we could master lasting sustainable energy if we paid attention to what we need. I usually have a green smoothie as soon as I'm hungry, typically around 10:00 or 11:00 A.M.

I love the concept of time-restricted eating. Unlike intermittent fasting, which involves caloric restriction, time-restricted eating allows us to eat during a day window, and I don't wait to eat too late. Ideally, I prefer not to eat after 8:30 P.M. I eat raw and cooked whole foods throughout the day. I also make sure I have plant-based proteins for lunch and dinner.

I enjoy testing and developing mind, food, and body rituals that connect us all with our body, authentic self, spirituality, and culture. My wellness practice allows me to connect with my inner source of strength, and my morning rituals are key for my mental, emotional, and physical performance.

As I mentioned before, my self-care practices are not a one-time deal. I see them as oxygen for the rest of our lives. They are vital supplements that build us up and can support us through the most challenging moments of our lives. I experienced this firsthand during grief, my physical decline, and traumatic mental health crises. Rituals are a life source and essential for brain, gut, body, mental, and emotional health.

What is the most worthwhile investment you have made for your business?

I hired the right accountability business coach who cares about my success, believes in me, and, more importantly, believes in the importance of my core message. Finding the person you connect with, who holds you accountable and gives you gentle nudges to keep taking action is essential.

My coach has been key in helping me get unstuck in projects and negative patterns. Through her support, I've deepened my understanding that a winning mindset is one where we understand that entrepreneurship is a lifelong process of pivots, reinventions, collaboration, support, and checking in with one's energy.

If you lost everything today, what would you do for the next thirty days to generate income?

If I lost everything today, I would offer one-on-one customized packages and offer small mini group coaching programs.

How can people connect with you?

I can be found at madresoul.com and on Instagram @aranzasudelao.

I SEE MY ROLE AS A LIFE COACH AS SOMEONE WHO HELPS MY CLIENTS TRAIN THEIR MINDS, EMOTIONS, AND SPIRITS, JUST LIKE A PERSONAL TRAINER WOULD HELP STRENGTHEN YOUR BODY.

Sarah Failla

CHAPTER 9

EMBRACE THE UNEXPECTED BY SARAH FAILLA

I never intended to be an entrepreneur. In most areas of my life, I feel confident and competent. But internally, when it comes to being an entrepreneur, I still frequently doubt myself. Even as I sit here to share my journey with you, there's a little voice in the back of my head telling me that I don't belong in this book with these women. That voice is asking me, *How did you sneak your way into this book?*

I don't have a college degree. I'm not a type A, go-go-go person. I don't always need things to be bigger and better. I like to keep things simple, and I don't want to create an empire. (Yes, I realize I am revealing many stereotypes I once held about entrepreneurs. Forgive me. What entrepreneur stereotypes do you have, and how might they hinder you from showing up as your true self?)

From the outside, no one would know this voice is always with me. I've learned to be okay with it and acknowledge that it may never leave. Each new level in my business brings new doubts. And I keep showing up. I don't usually let the little voice in my head win. And as I keep showing up, I build resilience.

The possibility that I could be an entrepreneur came when a friend lent me some workout DVDs, and I was finally able to lose the weight I had gained right out of high school. And it was empowering to learn how to make my workouts and meals work for me. I was living in China at the time, and the idea of starting a business, especially while living overseas, had never crossed my mind.

When I was seventeen, I graduated high school early and joined a Christian missions organization. I would spend the next fifteen years in ministry with them. I experienced incredible things, met amazing people, traveled to over forty countries, and saw lives impacted in powerful and practical ways.

But during all that, I was beginning to want more for our family financially. I did not want to end up like some people I saw in ministry, working for very little in their youth and then in their older years struggling to get by. Living out of suitcases and on very little money was rewarding, but I also wanted to start building stability for our future and our kids.

I had a lot of mindset drama and unhealthy religious beliefs about how to mix money and meaning. I was raised as if they were mutually exclusive, and I would need to choose one over the other. So I spent years choosing meaning over money, not knowing it was a choice that didn't need to be made.

So when I saw results (losing thirty pounds and feeling so much better in my body) from the Beachbody workout DVDs and realized that others were willing to pay to experience that as well, I decided to work with that company, which was the beginning of what would become my entrepreneurial adventure.

What was happening to my body and my confidence made a big difference in my life. I had gained thirty pounds right out of high school and spent the next ten years trying everything I could think of (which wasn't much!) to lose it. I didn't grow up knowing a lot about nutrition. I thought ice cream was a staple food group and that Mondays were official "diet starts over" day.

Between making a different kind of impact in my life and the lives of other women, along with financially contributing to my family, I knew having a business was for me. I began to love the excitement of creating systems to serve people in ways that immediately shifted things for them. I loved the satisfaction of seeing money and meaning coming together in ways I had never imagined possible.

We returned to the US in 2012, and I was still working as a coach with that company and doing well. While in China, I had built my customer base and team in the US using social media and began learning about other online forms of marketing. I had two young kids at the time, and I loved that I could work around their schedules, set my hours, and be free to travel as much as we wanted.

While I loved what I was doing with that initial company, I didn't like having limits on my earning potential that were dependent on other people doing their work. I also wanted clear boundaries with who got my time and at what price. I was also running so many women through my weight loss groups that I didn't know what happened to them after the group because I was on to get the next customer to get my small commission. I wanted to go deeper, with fewer women, and see long-term holistic transformation happen.

Beyond all the earning limitations, I knew I liked diving into the core issues of weight loss, but I *loved* to help my clients uncover *why* they weren't at their ideal weight. I was able to help them get to the root of what else was out of alignment in their lives that was manifesting through health.

I decided to get more training to be better equipped to help clients, and I knew I wanted to focus on moms. Weight loss would be a focus but not the sole focus. Through losing weight, my clients would learn how to manage their lives better.

From my own life and that of my clients, I also began to see that there was a window of self-discovery that happens when the youngest child finally enters school or around age forty for the moms. It's a new awakening, a time of discovery and maturing for many women. It's a very powerful season, and it's my favorite time to coach my clients.

I first got certified as a personal trainer and then went on to get certified as a life coach (ACC) and a health coach through Integrative Nutrition and Precision Nutrition. I also took courses on inner healing and the Enneagram. I'm not officially certified as a Gallup-Certified Strengths Coach (my husband is), but I've been using it for over fifteen years and know enough to incorporate it into my coaching.

I left that initial company and started my own coaching business as a life, health, and weight loss coach focused on helping moms. I was able to design a program that fit the length of time I wanted to work with them and get paid what I decided was fair, for my experience and expertise, and for them to be investing in themselves.

I fought my niche of weight loss for a *long* time. I didn't want to perpetuate a culture of body shame, but rather one of losing weight from a place of self-love and long-term health. It wasn't until I allowed myself to show up authentically and let my clients know that we would get the weight off through life coaching, mindset work, and inner healing that I started owning the niche of weight loss. If they just wanted a diet plan (which usually doesn't work in the long term), I wasn't the right coach for them.

Throughout this whole time, I also went through a massive theological shift. As I got older and had more life experiences, much of what I believed growing up didn't fit anymore. When your view of God doesn't fit in your box anymore, I've learned it's the box that's the problem, not God. And in my case, it was God inviting me out of the religious box that I had placed him/her in. Learning about paradoxes has radically changed my life. (More on that later.)

I love working on my business, and I love my clients. It's challenging and rewarding. That is how I unintentionally became an entrepreneur.

What is your *why* or purpose for your business?

"This is going to be extra heartbreaking," the doctor said as she waved the ultrasound wand over my belly. "There are two babies, but no heartbeats. I am so sorry." An hour earlier, my husband and I had been walking out the door, and he said, "Are you ready to see a heartbeat today?"

"Two heartbeats," I responded, because I knew there was more than one life growing inside me.

My husband and I miscarried our first baby, had our son Josh, miscarried the twins, miscarried two more babies, and then had Zac, and five years later, Nathan.

Life will be full of unexpected hard things, like losing babies, chronic illness, death, broken relationships, unraveling theologies that once grounded us, and the unseen, unspoken pain you silently carry. But life will also be full of unexpected beautiful surprises. These seasons will overlap. But you keep going. You build resilience. Through coaching, I have the privilege of helping my clients forge that resilience in themselves.

When I lost my babies, with the loss of the twins hitting me extra hard, I had so many questions for God. When your God box is small, it's easy to misunderstand or blame God or think your blessings are somehow because you've earned them. I had unintentionally built my life upon the idea that everything would always be okay if I was just a "good enough" human.

Those beliefs were also layered upon growing up in a church system where I was inundated with a thousand spoken and unspoken rules to live by, be judged by, assessed by, and ultimately controlled.

Be friendly, but not too nice because it could come across wrong. Be strong, but don't be a bitch or controlling. Smile, be pleasant, serve, put others before yourself. You are made in the image of God, but don't you dare refer to God as "she."

And I tried my best to follow all the rules. I was so busy trying to be good and do all the right things that I didn't even know who I was or what I wanted. I learned how to play small to avoid making mistakes. It was like my brain was hardwired or conditioned to play "Don't do anything risky that could get you in trouble" on repeat.

Frankly, it was exhausting. And I said, "Enough." And then clients who are also ready to say enough find me, and we start the journey. This kind of work takes time. I'm years into it, and I still find old programming coming up, so I dig up another lie or belief and keep moving forward.

I am learning to be free, to allow emotions, to make mistakes, to be human and divine.

It's not simply about trying to be good enough or to avoid "getting in trouble." It's about really engaging in the game of life. And that's what happens for my clients as well.

The purpose of my business has several layers. Life is complex. You are complex, and so is how we grow. At the core, I hold space that allows women to rewrite their identity in light of a more accurate, more holistic version of God and self.

And from that foundation, the coaching flows into better health habits, weight loss, mindset shifts, boundaries, confidence, relationships, personal and professional goals, and so much more. Embracing paradox is a crucial component of this journey.

A simple way to look at paradox is this: You are good, and you are capable of evil. You are divine, and you are human. You are a great mom, and you will cause your children pain. Embracing this begins to change how you see yourself, God, the world, and how you show up in it.

I support my clients in their lives, but many initially come to me for weight loss. Having struggled with my weight most of my life, I understand how frustrating and all-consuming it can be. Not being happy with your weight is exhausting.

It's emotionally exhausting because you're embarrassed and ashamed and fighting cravings that feel out of control. Clothes feel uncomfortable, and the mind games with the scale are maddening.

It's mentally exhausting because there is so much conflicting information. You don't know who to trust, so you constantly analyze if what you're doing is the "right thing." When you look at some of the myriads of diet and fitness plans out there, you wonder how any working mom has time for any of it!

I love to ask my clients, "Imagine if you never had to think about weight loss again. What would you do with all that time and energy?" I ask this because losing weight is about feeling healthy and strong, but it's also about getting back *into* your life. It's hard to believe how much time and energy I wasted thinking about diets or researching the next plan. Struggling to get the weight off after baby number three, I blamed it on being older, my metabolism, hormones, which are all good things to take into consideration. In my situation, though, which is the same for many of my clients, as you get older, you need to do a few things differently. The main one is trusting the process. Once I finally ate humble pie and took my advice and hired a long-term coach, I got the weight off. Having the support through the ups and downs and someone there to hold me accountable made all the difference.

Today, my weight loss coaching tool kit is massive. It has to be, because I don't believe in a one-size-fits-all diet/fitness plan. It combines health coaching and life coaching with mindset tools. I help clients learn to trust the process, ignore all the noise and quick fixes, listen to their body's needs, and figure out what works for them.

Working through weight loss will open the window into the other areas that need to and are ready to be healed. It doesn't happen overnight, but as I journey with these moms through the ups and downs of life, they begin to build inner confidence. Discipline. Resilience.

And what happens to a mom happens to a family. And that ripples out to the community, city, and every area of society. That's why it's an honor to work with moms.

Which activities do you perform that generate the majority of your revenue?

Working with clients one-on-one is the majority of my revenue.

What hard lessons have you learned that could have been avoided?

In my experience in the coaching industry, I had to learn (after spending lots of time and money) that while certifications are great, they will never give me the confidence that needs to be forged by actually coaching, by taking action. I still remind myself that certifications are enhancements. They are not the total solution to self-doubt.

What self-care, routines, and habits do you have to maintain good health?

"I don't know what a mental breakdown looks like, but I feel like I'm on the verge of one," I said to my husband in August 2014.

In the six months leading up to that, I had given birth to my third son, was diagnosed with stage five kidney disease, unexpectedly lost my dad to a heart attack (age sixty-three), and took a month-long trip back to China. Oh, did I mention my husband and I had just stepped in as pastors of a local faith community (all while I was in a massive theological deconstruction about what I even thought about God and church)?

In that conversation with my husband, I knew myself well enough to know this was an internal "I'm not okay" moment unlike any I had experienced before, and I needed outside help to move through it. There will be seasons of life when self-care requires reaching out and getting support from others.

Some people see self-care as an afterthought, some see it as a luxury, some see it as unnecessary, and some even see it as impossible. I see self-care as *preparation*. Whether it's in health, life, or business, it's not *if* the storms will come, but *when*.

Some storms will come without warning, like those six months in 2014 or through miscarrying five babies. And some storms we can prepare for, like the kidney transplant I will have later this year. In both scenarios, we have an opportunity today to set habits in place to help us build resilience for those seasons.

I see my role as a life coach as someone who helps my clients train their minds, emotions, and spirits, just like a personal trainer would help strengthen your body. And that strength helps us weather storms with courage.

In my coaching program, I support my clients through four main pillars of self, which all lead to improved life habits: The Body, Mindset/Identity, Relationships & Support. I use these same tools in my own life.

THE BODY: I can't stress this enough: If you neglect your body, it will demand payment at some point. The foundation of my health habits is:

- Go to bed on time. I always prioritize sleep, even over workouts.
- Drink water.
- Eat 80 percent on-point and healthy foods. Enjoy your food, fully present, with nothing to hide, guilt-free. No food is good or bad, and it's about choices that work for your body and your goals.
- Move your body in a way that feels good. I don't have a strict workout routine. Walking, spinning, weights. I get them in, but I listen to my energy levels as well.

Nourish and move your body from a place of love. If you want and need to lose weight, do it. If you don't, let it go and be free from that preoccupation.

If you are struggling with your health, start small—build in one new habit at a time. For example, go to bed twenty minutes earlier, add in five hundred extra steps each day, or swap out one soda for water.

If you struggle with overeating, ask yourself this: Where in your life do you feel out of control, stressed out, or that a boundary has been crossed? When we take away judgment and shame, our eating can be a window into what is going on in our lives, emotions, minds, and bodies.

THE FEMALE BODY: Don't ignore your cycle. Track it and understand how your hormones affect your energy, motivation, and physical capacity throughout the month.

MINDSET/IDENTITY: A daily brain dump is incredibly helpful when it comes to calming what could quickly become chaos in my full schedule and life with three school-age boys.

I write out everything I'm thinking into a journal without judgment. Self-awareness is the first step to setting boundaries, emotional regulation, confidence, and overcoming limiting beliefs. Start by being honest with where you are now (mentally, emotionally, physically, spiritually).

From there, I coach myself in a variety of ways using different tools. A few questions you can start with are:

- Do I believe this thought is true? Why or why not?
- Would I like to believe something different? If so, what?
- Where did I get this thought (a person, teacher, societal norm, etc.)? Do I still believe this to be true?

If you do this for thirty days, I guarantee you that you will grow.

Allow space for fears and shame to be exposed: *I'm not lovable, enough, too much, unworthy, etc.*, which, when brought into the light, will bring waves of freedom throughout your life.

RELATIONSHIPS & SUPPORT: Working on identity and mindset is key to healthy functioning and having healthy relationships. I am continually evaluating how I am showing up in my relationships. I'm very independent, and another life lesson I have learned from running my own business is that I can't do everything alone. A habit I have is asking myself these questions:

- Is there a boundary I need to set but am afraid of? Why? Who am I afraid of disappointing?
- Am I meeting my own needs with the same commitment that I meet the needs of others? Why or why not?
- Who do I have in my life supporting me to reach my goals?
- If I'm annoyed or judging someone, I ask what it is in that person that I don't like in myself or that I'm envious of.
- How does my business fit into the larger picture of my dreams and goals? Are there competing values between my business and family goals that need attention?

I also have a super-tight inner circle of friends to be 100 percent honest about anything and everything. We ask hard questions and give real answers. So, cultivate your community and especially your inner circle.

You can see I have a lot to say about self-care. The heart of my business is helping moms prioritize self-care so they can then have the physical, emotional, and mental energy to reach their goals while also being the mom they want to be.

Don't compare what self-care looks like for you with anyone else. Instead, it would be best if you evaluated (and consistently reevaluated) what self-care looks like for you as the seasons of your life, family, and business change and grow.

Investing time and money in your physical, mental, and emotional well-being is never a waste. If you want to bring your best to your business and your family, you must take this seriously. Don't believe the lie that something is wrong with you if you need support. It's part of being human.

What is the most worthwhile investment you have made for your business?

Learning how to manage my mind and emotions and coach myself. I've done this through hiring coaches and being in coaching programs. When I took ownership of the problems that had nothing to do with tactics and were because of my mindset, things began to change.

If you lost everything today, what would you do for the next thirty days to generate income?

I would tell everyone I contact that I am a life and weight loss coach and offer to help them. Practically, this would look like getting potential clients on the phone or Zoom for a consultation and then creating a plan to work together.

Social media is still my favorite way to meet clients and grow my business, so I would start there. Plus, I'd get a website going again, as I always want to be building for the long term.

How can people connect with you?

I can be found at momcoachsarah.com.

IT DOES NOT HAVE TO BE BEAUTIFUL TO START. YOU JUST HAVE TO GET IT OUT THERE.

Ashley Helene

CHAPTER 10

PIVOTING FOR SUCCESS BY ASHLEY HELENE

We all face some type of struggle or setback in our lives, and for me, many of those setbacks came in my career. After years of competitive swimming and triathlons, I finished college and planned to continue racing professionally. A few weeks after my decision, I was hit by a car while participating in a triathlon, breaking my jaw and destroying my bike. Thankfully, I survived and felt pretty good. Ten days later, I was back in the gym, but on the ride home (riding my mountain bike this time), I was hit by another car. This time I broke my back. I was extremely fortunate to still be alive. Because I was in good physical shape, I did not spend a single night in the hospital. I was released each time.

With my injuries and back-to-back accidents, I decided that maybe I was meant to do something else. At the height of an economic crisis in the United States in 2008, I was fresh out of college and had no work experience. When you go to college, you're usually guaranteed to find a job. That was not the case in a recession. I applied for job after job with no luck. No one was hiring. With nothing available, I started my entrepreneurial journey. I started with two jobs, one as a personal trainer and another with an internet marketing company. I spent ten to fifteen hours a week in traffic to and from the gym. I felt stuck. Being a personal trainer, you usually work in the mornings and the evenings. I dreaded coming back to the gym every day. I knew there was more to life than this daily grind.

I met my business partner, a flight instructor, who was commuting out to the airport and flight instructing one student at a time. We decided to combine our skills, my internet marketing skills, and my partner's flight instruction knowledge to create a program to reach students individually and in multiples. I built an online membership-based platform to reach students all over the world. I wanted to maximize my time and knew if I did that, I could have a life where I traveled and worked from anywhere. I could have a family and spend time with them. I was passionate about homeschooling my kids, so it was essential to making the best and most efficient use of my time.

When I started more than ten years ago, membership site software was limited at best, and I spent a lot of time coding and developing systems to provide the best membership experience. Membership sites weren't even a thing yet, but today they are extremely prevalent.

Best of all, you don't have to be a "techie." It's great if you are, but not a problem if you're not! I have been very blessed by sharing what I've learned over the years to help others create their membership sites. I've worked with fitness instructors, mechanics, marketing specialists, general education teachers, business coaches, and many more industry professionals.

What is your *why* or purpose for your business?

My most significant reason is my children: spending time with my children, not only raising them but homeschooling them, and getting to see the world through their eyes. For example, when my son was three months old, we took him to Europe. He got to visit Ireland, England, and Germany—a world traveler at three months old! The freedom to travel anywhere and not worry about work or the money coming in is fantastic.

Although I think for every mother, their children are a huge reason they do what they do, my *why* isn't just about my children. I love giving back and helping others succeed. I got so many requests to share what I was doing with our flight-training business that when it came time to sell that company, I went full-time into helping others create their membership sites. It gives me great pleasure to see others succeed. I've gone through all the struggles it takes to be an entrepreneur.

We got to a point when we started the flight-training business where we had to sell our airplanes. We spent several months teaching students to fly, and we didn't even own a plane. But we pushed through and kept working hard to be successful and eventually repurchased our first plane and five others for a total of six aircraft. I continue to share the failures and struggles I've gone through as a business owner to help others minimize the losses and struggles they encounter to reach their goals and be successful faster.

What are the biggest mistakes you see new entrepreneurs making?

Being in the online business space for over ten years, I see many mistakes that new entrepreneurs make along their journey. One of the biggest mistakes I see is not building an email list. Nowadays, with social media, it's easy to build a following on Instagram, Twitter, TikTok, Pinterest, YouTube, etc., which is excellent for your business. But we don't own those platforms. What if your account is hacked, reported, and banned one day, and you no longer have access to it? Would your business be able to survive if that just disappeared one day?

Many years ago, we did all our marketing on YouTube. YouTube was where our prospects were finding us at the time. We had a following of around one hundred thousand on the platform. One morning, we woke up to find out our account no longer existed. It was just gone. There was nothing YouTube could do to get it back. This is very common in today's world—not just hacking, but a media platform's ability to restrict or turn off your account if they don't agree with what you're posting. We had to start a new account with zero followers. The only way we survived was by having an email list.

Over the years, we built our email list by having customers and prospects opt in to receive more information on flight training. When we had to start a new YouTube account, we thankfully had all the videos saved—well, most of the videos. It was a long upload process, but we rebuilt our YouTube presence. After the new account was created, we emailed our list, letting them know what happened and how to find the new channel.

Thankfully, we had spent the time building an email list and were able to maintain our business with minimal loss. However, nowadays, it's more important than ever to build an email list. You see so many accounts getting shut down for no reason. So when you're just starting, I know you don't want to think about the bad things that could happen, but to grow a successful business, you must have backup systems in place to protect yourself and your company.

When entrepreneurs are just starting their businesses, I also see a lot of imposter syndrome and self-doubt. Imposter syndrome is a real thing that many entrepreneurs struggle with, which leads to them not starting the company of their dreams. It's important to get started. Nothing will happen if you keep planning without implementing.

I used to be part of a mastermind group, and we had monthly events where we invited entrepreneurs to a meeting to network and for coaching sessions to help them with their businesses. One lady still stands out to me. I'm sure she never started her business. She would show up each month with all her ideas, and when asked how her business was going, she would tell us she hadn't started taking on clients and hadn't released her product to the world. Each month she worked on her logo or on her business cards instead of getting her product out to the world.

It does not have to be beautiful to start. You just have to get it out there. For any entrepreneur, especially in the internet space, you can go back to their first videos, pictures, logos, and posts and see that it was less than perfect. As long as you provide value and service to your customers, it does not matter how it looks. You can update different aspects as you grow. For example, if you want to produce video content, don't wait until you have a big fancy video studio to begin. It's never going to happen. Instead, you can start with your phone by taking a selfie video to get your message out. In anything you do, it's crucial to implement right away and perfect it as you go.

Which activities do you perform that generate the majority of your revenue?

Generating revenue is a vital part of any business. If you're not generating revenue, you don't have a business. Every day, in order to generate income, I am constantly creating content and sharing it with my ideal clients. Depending on your business and where your ideal client hangs out is where you'll want to focus your time. For my flight-training company, our ideal client was on YouTube. We released weekly videos to reach them.

With that, we repurposed content. I highly recommend this to help you save time and money. Let's say it's a YouTube video you're creating. You create the video, post it to your YouTube channel, post the video to your blog, and create a blog post by having the audio converted to text. Highlights from the video can be used for social media posts. If you want to get creative, you can use the audio from the video for a podcast. When you create content, get creative and figure out ways to break it down and come up with different uses for it.

How have you diversified your revenue streams within your business?

Diversifying is extremely important to growing your business. By creating different areas within your business, you can continue to grow and reach different audiences. I recommend starting with one signature or core product. Then, when you have that core product set up and doing well, you can add additional product offerings and variations to reach different customer groups.

It's essential in the beginning to get very specific in your niche and then expand from there. To go back to my flight-training company, we started by only offering entry-level pilot training. When you're becoming a pilot, you go through different levels in your training. By creating the entry-level product (private pilot), we focused on clients beginning their flight-training journey to learn how to fly. Once our main customer base finished it, they started requesting the next level of certification. In this case, it was instrument pilot training. So we developed the next level course. The requests continued to come as students progressed through their program. We continued to add classes for all possible levels of certification and diversified our offerings.

After you have your core product, you can create different ways to reach more clients. Another example would be if you had a core product that was, let's say, a $10,000 coaching program. You attract your ideal client into the coaching program but still want to serve those who are budget conscious. That's a great time to create a low-end program where you can nurture those clients and build them up to join the core coaching program in the future. They can advance through your coaching program and move to your more advanced program. Creating a high-level mastermind would be a significant step up for those clients. That gives you at least three levels to work with, and you can continue to expand your offerings from there.

What is one of your greatest failures that ultimately led to success?

As an entrepreneur, you have a lot of failures. My most significant failure was trying to build an app to go along with our business. We spent somewhere between $20,000 to $30,000 (which is relatively cheap) developing our app.

It was a total flop. We released it and had a handful of users. The app had many bugs, and the price to keep it going was just as expensive as building the app. We had no way to monetize the app. We were losing money like crazy. We had to pull the plug and take it as a loss.

From that failure, I learned the importance of having a monetization plan in place. If you're putting out money for something that you think is a good idea, but it's not productive for your business, maybe the timing is off. Always focus on items that follow your core values and are going to grow your business. Don't always chase after ideas that sound good, because they are most likely too good to be true.

Another failure I had was having to sell our first airplane while running a flight-training company. Early on in our company, we were making money but not enough to afford essential items and invest in the company to keep it growing. Our airplane at the time required a new engine (it cost more than the airplane itself), and we did not have the money to afford it. We were barely getting by as it was. So, we had to sell the plane. With the airplane sale pending, we spent the last week filming a ton of videos to use in the future until we could purchase another airplane.

While we were airplane-less, we worked like crazy to keep the business steady with the hopes that it continued to grow. We wrote books and continued to publish the video content to YouTube that we grew slowly over time. Sure enough, the business continued to grow, and over time, we were able to buy another airplane.

I learned that no matter what you're going through, you'll find a way to be successful if you work hard and stay consistent. For example, we were teaching people to fly, and we didn't even have an airplane. By continuing to focus on helping others learn how to fly, we could keep going and reach our goals.

That's just one story of many failures I've had along the way in my entrepreneurial journey. When you're an entrepreneur, you have to learn to roll with the punches, as they say. You will not be successful at everything you do. But you have to learn to continue to move forward and learn from that failure.

What hard lessons have you learned that could have been avoided?

I should've hired employees sooner. When you start your business, it's your baby and you're doing all of the things. Hiring employees is scary because no one can do it like you. However, you'll find that you'll be more successful with someone doing it at 80 percent than you trying to do it all yourself. It can be confusing to know what position you should hire for when you're starting your business. The best plan is to hire where you need the most help and hire for things you dislike doing or take a lot of your time. Then, you can easily find someone who enjoys that job and can do it much more efficiently than you can do alone. Sometimes it's not always hiring someone within your business. For me, it was hiring someone to help maintain my house. I'm a single mother of two kids, and I don't enjoy cleaning the house. Hiring someone helps give me more time to focus on work and the things I enjoy doing.

With hiring, you have to learn how to hire slow and fire fast. When you're hiring, please get to know the person and make sure they are a good fit for your company and culture. You want to build a team that gets along and builds each other up. Having a bad employee can quickly bring the culture and business crashing down. When you get a bad apple in the group, be quick to fire and decide to let them go. It's not only your livelihood, but it's the livelihood of all the families you employ.

What self-care, routines, and habits do you have to maintain good health?

Health is a huge aspect when it comes to your business and life. It is imperative because, without good health, we can't do what we do, nor would we enjoy our lives. When we talk about health, it's not just physical health but also mental health. Mental health is just as vital as physical health, and many of us neglect it. A great example of this is Simone Biles in 2021 during the 2020 Tokyo Olympics, who was physically ready to compete but withdrew due to mental health. Most of us push through, just trying to keep going without taking a moment to think about how it is affecting our minds and bodies. We perform best when we are both mentally and physically ready for the challenge ahead.

Previously, I had been so deep in the weeds of my business that I had no time for myself. I struggled to do all the things—take care of the kids, provide their education, run the business. Once I learned how to step back and make time for myself, everything changed. I make time every day to work out in the mornings. It keeps me physically fit and gives that energy boost to help get me through the day. For mental health, I plan once a month to have a spa day or shopping day—one day just for myself. I usually go and get a pedicure and manicure, but some days I'll take a shopping day to find something new while not worrying about work or anything else that might be going on. Just time to relax and recharge to take on the daily struggles and stress we all go through.

If you lost everything today, what would you do for the next thirty days to generate income?

That is a great question and something that I went through recently. Of course, you never plan to lose everything and start over, but it does happen all the time, especially when you least expect it. In my case, I lost not only my husband, but I lost my business to divorce. That was the hardest for me. My business was my baby; I had put my entire life into it, and it showed. We bootstrapped from nothing to a multimillion-dollar company and landing on *Inc. Magazine*'s 5000 Fastest-Growing Companies list for three consecutive years. After days of tears and pulling myself together, I had to think of what I wanted to do with my life. Finally, I had a clean slate to work with and started over from scratch.

After reflecting on everything, I came back to my love of tech and helping others. Thinking back to over twelve years ago, building a membership site before membership sites were a thing, and loving every aspect of building the tech side and automation, I decided to help others create their membership sites. I developed my ideal client avatar, narrowed down my niche, and created a program to help entrepreneurs take and grow their businesses online by creating their community site.

I began creating content and sharing it on social media. As I mentioned earlier, I often see people have an idea for a business but never get started. I like to take the tech burden off the entrepreneur and create a system that works quickly and effectively for what they're trying to accomplish. I also wrote my first book called *Membership Site Success* to reach my ideal clients. I'm so happy to work with hundreds of entrepreneurs and to share my experiences so they don't have to go through as many bumps and issues along their road to entrepreneurship.

How can people connect with you?

I can be found at mgbizconsulting.com and on Instagram @mgbusinessconsulting.

TO THIS DAY, DECADES LATER, WHEN I'M NOT GETTING THE RESULTS I WANT, I TURN INSIDE FIRST AND CHECK IN WITH WHAT NEEDS TO BE HEARD, HELD, OR HEALED.

Lani Dickinson

CHAPTER 11

TIME FOR WHAT MATTERS BY LANI DICKINSON

"You're like a bull in a china shop, and if you want to be an executive, you're going to have to learn to be a lot nicer."

That is what the 5′3″ mafioso-looking male CEO sitting across the characteristically huge corporate desk said to me as his CoverGirl makeup cracked in anger at my latest direct assessment and even more direct solution to whatever problem we continued to never solve—mainly because we could never really say what was really wrong.

I get it. I shouldn't have been telling old white men to go fuck themselves in the boardroom, but at the end of the day, I was in my midthirties and just sick of knowing what was wrong but implementing purely stupid plans that the men (who were a big part of the problem) came up with because it was the late 1990s and I had boobs and a pretty face, so I was supposed to stay quiet and play nice.

Well, the way I grew up didn't lend itself to playing nice. You see, my mom was a street drug dealer for some portion of her adult life, and that overlapped with my early childhood years. I won't go into all the gory details, but I will recap a few key things from my second-grade year to help with understanding where my lack of boardroom manners may have originated. To start, I wouldn't bring any friends home from school to play like the other kids did for a few key reasons:

1. There was very likely going to be a pile of uncut cocaine on the living room table.
2. The cop who lived with us and rode with us to the Blue Moon Café to pick up the drugs often left his gun on his bed or the dresser, and his door was always open.
3. It wasn't uncommon to try to open the door to where we "lived" to find out either the house had been ransacked and everything was upside down (and my shoes stolen), or we didn't live there anymore.

Suffice it to say, many of the things you might imagine happening to a little girl who grew up that way happened, and it was best not to risk bringing any normal kids over to play. Through high school, I would hear, "Lani, you can come over here, but [insert name] can't go to your house."

With that beginning, it is by the grace of God, the love of my grandmother, my love for my son and our security, and a few dedicated mentors that I became a nurse with an MBA who then climbed the corporate ladder to become CEO of a company that is referred to in the press as a Fortune 175 company.

That level of success would not have been possible without that male CEO making it clear to me what was on the line. He also said, "Lani, you are *by far* the smartest person I have ever worked with, and I am retirement age. You are going to throw your future away if you don't get this behavior cleaned up. You have to learn how to be nice!"

But I *was* nice!

Even though I had received this feedback a bajillion times in my life, I had never gotten any confirmation on what "nicer" but not a "total airhead or pushover" looked like. (I was not only mouthy, but I was also quite judgy.) This particular episode of *Be Nicer* was scary for me because I was reading between the lines that my job security was at risk at this point. I had to do something different, so I searched for someone who could help me unpack and decode what "being nicer" meant in terms of actionable behaviors that still got results, because I am all about results.

I ended up in executive finishing school with my first high-ticket coach getting my colors done, learning how to use the utensils at a meal, and how to walk downstairs in high heels and a boa. While the whole week seemed like a true WTF moment, and I kept thinking, *How in the hell is this going to make me successful?* at the end of the week, I received the next most valuable piece of coaching of my life from the group leader Gloria.

She said, "You come off as cold and uncaring, and I can see you've been hurt, and it isn't safe to trust anyone, but have you thought about who else may be suffering from your approach? It's not all the job and security, Lani." Not only did she nail me, but she also gave me actionable behaviors and ways of communicating that I could implement immediately at work and at home.

I implemented everything she said immediately, and I also found an NLP (neurolinguistic programming) coach near me and went on an incredible healing journey for the next few years. I dealt with all the stuff and had amazing results, including getting a promotion every eighteen to twenty-four months after that . . . all the way to the top!

I wanted those kinds of results for anyone and everyone, no matter what their opportunity was. Thus, a transformational coach and my company, Thrive.OnPurpose., was born. Long story short: side-hustle coaching on anything for anyone who showed up was rewarding but quite exhausting. And very hard to sell.

The next leg of the journey had me $450,000 into coaches and courses and programs learning how to grow and scale a business online. It started with an ad that said they would help me fill my empty event rooms. Yes, I needed that! So I went all in on the $50,000 inner circle offer. I left that experience knowing how to sell from the stage—though still not knowing how to fill the room—but clearer than ever that I had to learn to sell online.

I thought I got smart when I asked for a reference. I called someone I knew and said, "Hey, I need to figure out how to sell online. Who do you trust?" This landed me in a $60,000 funnel-done-for-you yearlong program that taught me automated webinars, and the coach told me I wasn't selling on the webinars because I had to lose my corporate story. I rerecorded that thing five times in between cold calls to friends and family for clients because it just wasn't working.

And then the moment came when I realized I had to do something different. The done-for-you funnel was delivered, and the builder said, "It's ready for you to put the copy in." Copy? Back then, I didn't know how to write copy. I just wanted to help people heal and transform their lives. Wasn't the copy on the funnel part of the $60,000 done-for-you package? Of course, you know the answer was no. So I needed to find a solution for how to write copy that converted. At that moment, I knew I had to stop hiring coaches and just start doing and implementing whatever I had learned up to that point. So I did just that.

I spent two years focused on figuring out how to sell online—on my own. I tested everything in my live event and coaching businesses and the boot camp gym I owned. I had already bought all the courses and programs I could find on automation, sales, digital marketing, and copy. I grew both my coaching company and that little gym to multiple six figures each year before COVID-19 hit. With this success, I was planning on quitting my corporate job on my forty-ninth birthday, but two weeks before the planned date, California went on lockdown and I felt I had to focus only on being a hospital CEO. What nurse leaves when that kind of batter erupts? Not this one. So I stayed.

Two weeks later, my attorney husband came home and proclaimed he was busier than ever, which I thought was great given the lockdown. He quickly corrected me. The surge in his business was domestic violence and child abuse cases, and that was nothing to celebrate.

It was like an instant download came to me. I had all these years of being the corporate turnaround and growth strategist. I had grown both my companies to multiple six figures and was on track for seven figures, all in a very short period. I was also behind-the-scenes of my husband's law practice survival and growth in the 2008 downturn. Women and their kids across the globe were now at risk to become vulnerable due to the lockdown, and I had everything they needed to either start up or shore up their businesses so they would never have to rely on a corporation, a job, a boss, or someone else to pay the bills or take care of their kids.

A Woman's ONLY Business Coach was born, and I put my first six women entrepreneurs through my Next 100K program during COVID-19. There were fantastic results in that group, so I continued and created my Concept 2 Commas Rapid Business Growth Accelerator, where I help female service-based entrepreneurs scale their businesses online. My women call themselves #CommaMakers for the two commas they are creating in their bank accounts!

What is your *why* or purpose for your business?

The bottom line for why I do what I do is this: I want women to never have to rely on a corporation, job, boss, or someone else to pay their bills. I want women never to have to be compromised in their decisions about their kids or their families. So, I help them to build a business that gets them time freedom, financial freedom, and the ability to build generational wealth while never missing a moment that matters. I have the same *why* for myself—and my business gives me all of these things, so now I focus on helping others have it all too!

What are the biggest mistakes you see new entrepreneurs making?

Spending time and money on things like logos and branding, which could put them out of business before they even truly get started, rather than spending time and money getting clear on what their ideal clients will pay for. They also don't get visible soon enough or in a big enough way, or they don't do what it takes to get their first five *real* clients fast enough. These are all critical mistakes.

The other thing I see new entrepreneurs do that detracts from their success is thinking the "next thing" will be the answer, so they chase bright shiny objects and patch together all the tiny offers rather than dig in, understand their customers and the market deeply, and then learn how to sell in that space. The truth is, many strategies can and will work, but they must be fully implemented, tested, tweaked, and optimized based on results, and then finally mastered. That all takes time, investment, and stick-to-it-ness. I see too many entrepreneurs not implementing at that level before they add on a new tactic. There are no overnight solutions, and businesses do not get to a million dollars overnight. When the newer entrepreneur doesn't realize this and chases the next thing that sounds good, it pulls their time, attention, and money away from meaningful investment. And *that* gets them to stop the proverbial three feet short of gold.

Which activities do you perform that generate the majority of your revenue?

I generate the bulk of my revenue by running live challenges in my Facebook group. For example, I created and run the free High-Ticket Client Attraction Bootcamp every six to eight weeks in the Woman Entrepreneur Launch, Grow, Scale & Thrive Facebook group. This leads to a one-year high-touch full business incubator called the Concept 2 Commmas Rapid Business Growth Accelerator.

What is one of your greatest failures that ultimately led to success?

At the time I was heading to executive finishing school, I was failing miserably internally. I had failed to recognize the toll my early years, and my survival instinct, had taken on me. As I was climbing the ladder, I underappreciated how much the trauma of my early years would impact me, my career, and my important relationships. Those early years silently, but not without damage, fueled my drive for security even though I was safe and making more than enough money to take care of everything. I wrongly interpreted my earnings capability and my intact marriage to mean I was fine, and I just kept climbing at almost any cost.

Well, I wasn't fine. While the patterned behavior that was showing up in the workplace was a problem, it also impacted the relationships I cared most about in my personal life. Getting a coach for my mindset and healing issues was the best thing I ever did for myself and my important relationships. This was more important than any of the business coaching I ever paid for.

To this day, decades later, when I'm not getting the results I want, I turn inside *first* and check in with what needs to be heard, held, or healed. That didn't come naturally to me, but now I completely understand that I need to stop and take care of those issues before trying to do anything else. As a result, I have built this learning and capability into my business coaching programs.

So many business coaching programs have a chapter or module on mindset. And a mindset coach or program can certainly help you be more effective in business. But it takes so much more than that, and yet it's pretty rare to have a coach who can fully navigate both sides of that equation, but I can and do! I am certified in all things NLP, so I like to say I am a badass in business and I have a side of woo because I do recognize solid business strategy alone doesn't work well. It doesn't scale without an intact human on the other side of that strategy!

What hard lessons have you learned that could have been avoided?

When I was in the $60,000 done-for-you program, the coach kept telling me the reason I couldn't make sales was that I wasn't "shedding the corporate." I wasn't sure how to do that, as I had been in corporate for almost two decades at that point. I have learned that my people love my background and the credibility that goes along with being a Fortune 175 woman CEO, a nurse with an MBA, and a serial entrepreneur. My intended people I get the best results for all dig every piece of that. The pain of this almost two-year experience could have been avoided if I had just believed I was already good enough as I was. While I did have to do the work, I never had to shed any part of me, and you don't either!

What is the most worthwhile investment you have made for your business?

Team! Hands down, hiring a team is the best investment I have made in my business. I didn't get to the top of a Fortune 175 by doing everything myself! But when I applied that same logic to my entrepreneurial businesses, they grew by leaps and bounds!

I first invested in the things I didn't enjoy doing—like actually building the funnels. Then, I hired someone who loves the tech side of things and reinvested my time into consultation calls and closed clients and their results! Then I invested in the team to do the things that were important but repetitive and too numerous to keep up with in a timely manner—like emails, scheduling, and support tickets.

The parts that were hard to start sharing with team members were those I enjoyed and felt were a big part of the business success, *but* I also know my genius zone is in strategy development and the one-on-one coaching in the delivery portion of the business. That's where the clients get their best results, and that's what I'm known for and what they care about.

If you lost everything today, what would you do for the next thirty days to generate income?

If I lost everything today, on day one, I would remind myself that I could get a job as a nurse working three days a week for the next thirty days to generate the security income if I needed to. This would help me not to freak out or activate my security programming.

Then on day one, I would get really clear on what I wanted instead of the situation I had just been dealt and exactly my part in getting there so I wouldn't repeat it. Then I would get a clear picture of where I wanted to be in thirty days, ninety days, and one year from now. I would first write it all down and then start visualizing *all* of it—being grateful for it as if I already had all of it. I would hold this image in my mind constantly, and at least twice a day, I would deliberately and out loud read my written goal and then run through the details of the pictures of it in my mind.

Next, I would get clear on what I owed and what my options were for starting over. I would get all of this written down in one place and contact everyone I owed money to and let them know the situation I was in. I would let them know I was not avoiding them and that they would be paid so they didn't start calling me and dragging down my mindset and energy during my thirty-day sprint.

In the meantime, I would figure out what high-ticket problem I could solve that people were currently investing in. I would research this problem and make sure other people successfully sell products to solve this problem in the marketplace. I would be asking a lot of questions and getting clear on their pain points and their desires so I could put together an offer that would solve those problems that my ideal client at the time would invest in.

If I had nothing and no resources, this would be something that required nothing other than my time and my brain to implement; therefore, that would be in the mindset, healing, leadership, team development, executive, or business coaching spaces. I would want to pick one I liked enough to keep building for the future.

For me, that would be high-ticket business coaching one-on-one and group coaching; for the sake of this, I'm going to assume helping people make more money more quickly in their company will always be a hot and marketable skill set.

Once I was clear on that, I would hop on a free Canva account and start making all the collateral needed to allow my social media funnel to start funneling people to me, because the next step I would take is to start getting visible quickly; thus, I need these assets to make me look legitimate. I would also get my free Zoom account set up so that as soon as I have my first clients, I could record our sessions and save those for the program I'm building. I'm assuming that since I lost everything, I don't have enough money for a funnel builder yet, so I'm going to be sending people into a free Facebook group with a welcome video and some other excellent and relevant consumable video content to begin our relationship.

I would be going live and posting and giving value daily on my social channels and sending people to my free group and inviting them into consultation to see how I could help them. I would also be asking lots of direct questions about the problems my ideal client has and listening deeply in any forum where my ideal client was already congregated. I would start telling lots of stories on social media about the problems my potential clients were facing and delivering value on those pain points to get results, which would lead my community to know, like, and trust me.

I would also be reaching out to every person I had ever served in any way to ask for referrals and testimonies on how I had impacted their life or business. For the first three to five clients, I would offer a bargain-basement no-brainer investment for one-on-one high-ticket coaching, so they would just have to say yes, which would get me a cash infusion. For my next ten or so clients, I would offer just the no-brainer investment for one-on-one coaching or a six-week group coaching program. For all of these first clients, I would go all in and get them results (no matter what) so they would turn into testimonials and referrals as well as a cash infusion to fund the next leg of my journey, which includes the rest of the tools needed to grow an online business to scale fully.

All along the way, I would need to keep up with my daily workouts, even if they were only twenty minutes. Along with my workouts, I would need to keep up with my three liters of water to stay hydrated and healthy. Of course, it also goes without saying that I would need to keep up with my twice-daily visualization process and my daily spiritual practice.

How can people connect with you?

I can be found at Lani@LaniDickinson.com or in my Facebook group: Woman Entrepreneurs Launch, Grow, Scale & THRIVE!

THE MOST IMPORTANT THING THAT I DO TO TAKE CARE OF MY BODY AND MY SOUL IS NOT TO WAIT UNTIL I GET TIRED TO REST.

Emmy Hernandez

CHAPTER 12

A BUSINESS WITH HEART BY EMMY HERNANDEZ

I grew up in a very traditional Mexican household, and I watched at least five hours a day of telenovelas (Mexican soap operas). Also, I was obsessed with all the Disney princesses. Ariel was my favorite.

So, from a very early age, I knew *exactly* what love was! I had to turn myself into exactly what men wanted. That was easy. Glad I figured that out by the time I was fourteen. As the eldest of seven children, I grew up to be a huge bossy pants. And no, I don't mean that I was independent and empowered. I would boss everyone around: my siblings, my dad, my teachers. In one short sentence, I was a bitch.

It worked in my favor for many years when it came to schoolwork and even in my first few jobs. Being strong, independent, and opinionated were characteristics that everyone in my high school and university valued. I was praised for it. Here's why:

I'm the first person in my family to finish elementary school.

I earned a full-ride scholarship to UC Berkeley at age seventeen and had to forge my mom's signature to accept my offer because I was underage and my mom did not want me to leave the house.

Being the rebel that I was, I convinced my parents to drop me off on campus, and I swore I didn't need them anymore.

I cried for an entire week. I was no longer the boss of my high school. I was on a campus full of sharks, and I felt like a guppy trying to eat the scraps that everyone else left for me. College was not easy for me. I struggled *a lot* my first year but quickly picked up the pace and graduated with a high GPA in three and a half years. I went on to a corporate job as a marketing coordinator and eventually started my own marketing firm.

And then failed miserably. My professional failure humbled me, and I was devastated because I wasn't sure how to get back on my feet. During this time, I met someone. An amazing man who was at a personal development conference. This was the beginning of my demise. I had already experienced a great boyfriend in college, but I was bored with him after three years (remember, I told you that I was a bitch). I had one boyfriend for three months after that, and then I met this man who would become my greatest life lesson. Our romance was sexy, passionate, incredible, soulful, intellectual. We had a very special connection. I couldn't explain it.

And then, once I was madly in love with him, things started changing. He bought me a promise ring, so then I was committed to making this relationship work no matter what. He became extremely jealous of any communication I had with anyone other than him. I did everything wrong in his eyes, and he would explain it in such logical terms that I believed him. I moved in with him and disappeared to the rest of the world. I was always terrified of doing anything that he disapproved of.

Honestly, I was terrified of him. He had been to jail due to slapping his previous girlfriend, but he had convinced me that it was her fault. And again, I believed him. He convinced me to merge our financial accounts, and then he stopped paying my phone bill. I lost that phone number and still have no idea what happened to many of my friends, as I lost contact with them. Everything revolved around him and his dreams to be an international motivational speaker. Everyone swooned when they met him and told me how lucky I was to be with him. I believed them.

Behind closed doors, he was a different person, and I sincerely questioned my sanity. I was able to get out of this relationship after two years of torture. I have since recognized his behavior as narcissism, and I now know that I was a victim of a toxic abuser. He love-bombed me and then turned things around on me and made himself the victim of every situation. This is called gaslighting.

Since this experience, I dedicated my time to study neuroscience, quantum physics, love blueprints, the male versus female brain, and anything I could get my hands on that helped me understand what happened to me and how to stop it from *ever* happening again. I stopped being so aggressive in my life with people and with myself. I kicked perfectionism to the curb. I started being kind to myself, and truly, for the first time in my life, I could say, "I love myself." I learned the power of feminine energy and lived in it more often when it came to romance than my masculine energy (which was very helpful in corporate America, yet exhausting).

Once I broke out of the toxic spell, I became a renowned lean start-up coach in the tech industry and coached many entrepreneurs at different universities worldwide on how to launch and fund their start-ups. Microsoft and Lyft also hired me to come in and train their teams on powerful communication tactics. I became the translator between what people said and what people meant.

As my confidence grew back, I hired love coaches, and they helped me shift my love blueprint to something healthier. I began to live a life of so much fun, joy, and ease as a single woman. Then, in September 2017, I met the love of my life, Matt. He truly is the most incredible man and is beyond anything I imagined my life with my soul mate would be. We live like royalty. He is my king, and I am his queen.

For two years, I only told our story in private for fear of judgment. For two years, I kept all my secrets to myself. Many friends approached me to help them find soul-mate love, and they hired me to help them. I only did this as a hobby because I didn't think I could do this for a living. I laugh now just thinking about that limited mindset.

I got certified in different modalities, but the two most important ones that I use in my daily coaching are NLP (neurolinguistic programming) and superconscious recodes. I don't expect my clients to rely on willpower to change their programming, so we use science-backed techniques that change the coding in the brain for healthy love, not toxic love.

Now my business is global and booming. I have helped many women around the world attract, keep, and cocreate love relationships. I am honored to help many couples as well who come to me for relationship coaching.

I know in my soul that being a love and relationship coach is not a profession for me. This is my calling. This is my life's purpose. Other than the daily love I receive from Matt, there is no greater feeling than a message from one of my clients telling me the incredible news about their upcoming wedding with their soul mate. I know it's cliché, but my mess in love truly has become my message for the world.

What is your *why* or purpose for your business?

I'm on a mission to create a love paradigm shift on the planet. For thousands of years, women and men did not marry for love; marriage was a business transaction. In our modern-day era, marriage is mostly an agreement between two people who love each other and who come freely to the decision to join their lives together. However, the divorce data shows that so many marriages are failing, and even worse, those who stay married are mostly miserable. Is that the fault of marriage? No. It's that we haven't updated the institution to include *true* and needed communication skills, as well as recognizing our programming and core values.

So many couples "fall in love" based on the void they feel in their hearts and souls without realizing that once that initial glow of the relationship wears off, it quickly becomes a business transaction, where both parties keep track of what the other is doing for the relationship. This is not healthy love.

I'm on a mission to help millions of people on the planet reprogram their unconscious minds to attract healthy, incredible partnerships into their lives. This is not done through willpower. It's done through superconscious recoding and learning advanced communications skills for romantic partnership.

I'm here to help female empaths who have been or are currently victims of narcissistic, toxic partners. I'm here to help them heal and reprogram their brain and heart to create boundaries and only bring in healthy love with a partner who loves, respects, and cherishes them. This, beyond anything else, is what I will be doing until my dying breath—showing women and couples the light of true love. No manipulation. No games. Just pure, joyful, playful, and wholesome love.

What hard lessons have you learned that could have been avoided?

Filing for bankruptcy at age twenty-five, even when I didn't need to. I had some debt accumulated, but nothing that couldn't have been paid off easily with a consolidated loan or a settlement. I didn't know these things at the time. My ex-boyfriend convinced me to file for bankruptcy because he had already filed for bankruptcy the year before.

Lesson learned!

Another lesson I learned the hard way was hiring a coach who bullied me into buying her program. I knew something was wrong while on the sales call, but she convinced me she had what I wanted. Very early on in the group training, I did not appreciate her coaching style. She was way too aggressive for my taste—and not just with me. She made several women cry in training sessions and not in the "Wow, I just realized something" kind of way, but in the way of being a big egotistical bully. I should have trusted my intuition on the sales call and not let her push me or bully me into signing right on the spot. I fired her two months later and never looked back. That was a costly mistake, but I'm glad I learned it early on in my business.

What self-care, routines, and habits do you have to maintain good health?

The most important thing that I do to take care of my body and my soul is not to wait until I get tired to rest. I plan my rest. I work only Monday through Friday, and I don't do any coaching calls until 10:00 A.M. One day a week, I sleep in and don't do any coaching calls at all. I spend time meditating, reading, writing at a coffee shop (how else do you think I had time for this book?), and take myself out to lunch or meet up with a friend. I also alternate my schedule with yoga and a massage. One major thing that I did to take care of myself was outsourcing cleaning, laundry, and cooking. I have a wonderful woman who takes care of all that for me so that my love and I can spend more time together and I can focus 100 percent on my clients. I recently hired an executive assistant who takes all of the admin tasks off my plate and allows me to stay in my genius as a coach.

What is the most worthwhile investment you have made for your business?

It was investing in two incredible coaching programs only three months apart. I signed up with a large mastermind that helped me create the overall strategy of my business and formed my group program. Once I got my confidence in my niche and my expertise in the market, I hired another coach to help me create high-ticket offers and sell them without having to sell them. This has been the key to my success. It was investing in coaching before I had the money to invest. I got a small loan from my brother to make the initial deposit for the first program, and the rest is, as they say, history!

If you lost everything today, what would you do for the next thirty days to generate income?

I would create a free three-day training on Facebook where I invited people in my target market to attend the free sessions. Then I would invite them to a yearlong coaching program with me to create monthly recurring revenue.

How can people connect with you?

I can be found at dualityofathena.com and by email at Emmy@dualityofathena.com.

IT IS AN HONOR AND A PRIVILEGE TO WALK WITH WOMEN ON THEIR PATH TO BLOOMING. IT IS MY LIFE'S WORK.

Elizabeth Hambleton

CHAPTER 13

BRAVE ENOUGH TO BLOOM BY ELIZABETH HAMBLETON

Are entrepreneurs born or made? I can't say for certain, and perhaps it varies from person to person. Some of us probably have a personality that lends itself to the Wild West nature of blazing our own trail in business, while others are forged into entrepreneurs by life's twists and turns.

For me, it was the former. I wasn't surrounded by entrepreneurs or anyone who had a particularly firm grasp on concepts like growth mindset, abundance, or manifestation. Yet the notion of entrepreneurship has always magnetized me in a way I can't fully explain. Little did I know when getting started that it would take me nearly a decade to realize my dream of working for myself.

It's funny how some days in your life seem mundane at the time, yet they are the quiet beginnings of big things to come. I have an oddly crisp remembrance of one such day in college. I was sitting on my dorm room bed looking at an issue of *Lucky* magazine. They had done a feature on a woman who worked in fashion marketing, and her life seemed so inspiring and glamorous. I knew I wanted a creative career working for myself, but I also had the immediate realization that I didn't have the slightest idea how to create that type of life for myself.

So I did what most deeply practical people do. I got a steady job immediately after graduating from college. I was fortunate to find a position in an incredible art museum where I was surrounded by creative people and fun projects. I worked in the publishing department, and that's where I was first introduced to the world of graphic design and branding. While I did love many aspects of that job, it only took me a few years there to realize that while this line of work checked some of the boxes, it would never give me the creativity and freedom I craved.

Newly married at this point, I thought that perhaps sacrificing creativity for more money would be a better way to provide for my family. Unfortunately, that thought resulted in a brief and deeply misguided foray into the world of telecom. An early-stage cancer diagnosis during my first pregnancy sent me into a mild quarter-life crisis. How had I strayed so far from my original goals? It was time to get back on track.

A renewed vow to put creativity above financial gain led me into the fashion industry as a personal stylist. Once again, I landed a position that seemed good on paper and came with some nice perks (hello, shopping discount!), but it was ultimately not going to allow for the professional growth I wanted. The pay was also nothing to write home about, so I started picking up branding and design work as a side hustle for extra cash.

The more I connected with other female entrepreneurs struggling with their brand, the more I realized that merging the worlds of branding and personal styling would allow me to offer something unique and really special. And that's how Bonjour Branding was born.

Helping you feel amazing about the design of your brand is cool, but helping you feel confident about showing up in your brand is way more powerful. So many women are running amazing businesses, but they are sabotaging their success by not stepping into their role as the confident and empowered CEO.

When people think of branding, they often think of just the logo or the graphic design, but it's so much more than that. An entrepreneur's brand is powerful when it reflects and magnifies the beauty and strength of the person running the business.

You have so much beauty inside of you. If you've been hiding or holding back in your business (or from even starting a business), it's time to let the world see how beautiful you are. Design is just the first step in branding. The magic happens when you find the courage to be visible and let the world see your true self.

Whether you feel like you were born to be an entrepreneur or you just kind of fell into it, this journey is such a powerful one of self-discovery. The more you can make it about the inner work, the more you will thrive.

What is your *why* or purpose for your business?

The interesting thing about entrepreneurship is that it tends to amplify both your strengths and weaknesses. There are very few checks and balances in place as there would be in most traditional jobs, so you're left to make your own decisions without restraint. You are the sole determiner of your destiny. I find that so thrilling.

It speaks to my core personality. It's perhaps no surprise that I'm an eight (Challenger) on the Enneagram scale. The Enneagram Institute defines the key traits of an Eight as self-confident, decisive, willful, and confrontational.[1] (If you aren't familiar with the Enneagram, it's a personality test that helps you uncover your natural strengths and weaknesses.)

As a very extroverted Eight, putting myself in the spotlight has never (or at least very rarely) been a source of discomfort. Want me to be on your podcast? Perfect! Need me to make a speech in front of a group? No prob! Am I the person to show up in a bold outfit

---

[1] Type eight. (n.d.). Retrieved June 01, 2021, from https://www.enneagraminstitute.com/type-8

other people would think is crazy? You bet I am! Not only do I do these things, but I actually enjoy them. As I have gotten to know more and more women entrepreneurs, I have found that enjoying the spotlight is often not the norm.

In the past six years, I've had the honor of working with a really diverse group of women. Between personal styling and branding, I have now worked with over ten thousand clients. They have covered every inhabited continent as well as the complete spectrum of age, size, socioeconomic status, career ambitions, and pretty much any other demographic.

As different as these women were, I was struck by how much they were the same. So many of them struggled with confidence. They hid their true self, never feeling like they were ready for more. Unkind words spoken long ago, limiting beliefs picked up from past failures, and unmet expectations all served to weigh them down and keep them playing small.

I realized that helping women *look* better made them *feel* better. It was an instant way to share with them a valuable bump in confidence. You have probably experienced this yourself. Even the terms "power suit" or "little black dress" imply that you will feel different in those items than you would in baggy sweats.

I once had a client come to me looking for help getting dressed for her upcoming TED Talk. She was already a powerhouse in her field, yet she felt anxious about being judged by her appearance. Working with me wasn't really about the clothes. I could have chosen any number of dress and jacket combos for her. It was about making her *feel* a certain way. I was about making her feel confident and powerful and ready to go out there and kill it.

Clothes and graphic design can serve a very similar purpose. They both give a woman the confidence to show up and go bigger in her life. In the same way, a great outfit makes you feel more confident on a first date. A lovely brand can make you more confident when hosting your first webinar.

But I don't believe in stopping there. The outward transformation is just the start. It can be the tipping point that leads into the inner work. Because when you feel ready to take on the world, you show up with a different energy. And that can be such a powerful shift in your life.

The good news is that you don't have to be born with confidence to develop it. You just have to find the courage to bloom. As Anaïs Nin says, "And then the day came when the risk to remain tight in a bud was more painful than the risk it took to blossom."[2] It is an honor and a privilege to walk with women on their path to blooming. It is my life's work.

What are the biggest mistakes you see new entrepreneurs making?

One of the ironies about starting a business today is that it has never been easier, but it has also never been more confusing. There are countless experts and gurus, each trying to sell you their way to launch your dream business. While probably most of those people are well-intentioned, it leaves new entrepreneurs feeling paralyzed by choice. Everyone says that they know the way, but who can be trusted?

As a direct result of all that endless internet noise, I see one really common mistake: many new entrepreneurs don't sell anything. How does that happen? They get so caught up in setting up the trappings of a business (websites, logo, brand, etc.) that they end up missing the forest for the trees.

The core of your business needs to be an irresistible offer. Playing around with your website, logo, or social media may be fun, but it won't pay your bills. Many people starting are both unclear on their product messaging and scared of putting themselves out

---

[2] Risk by Anais Nin. (n.d.). Retrieved June 01, 2021, from https://allpoetry.com/poem/8497015-Risk-by-Anais-Nin

into the world to sell because they fear rejection. What happens when you combine those two things? You don't make any offers.

If you don't sell anything, you have a hobby or a charity. It's not a business. It's easy to get discouraged by the lack of money coming in and think that this whole "business thing" is either impossible or not for them. This is why so many businesses fail in their first year.

I see this tendency all the time in the world of branding. People spend months agonizing over the perfect logo or the perfect shade of pink. They think these are the critical business decisions that will convey some magic connection with their dream customer. I'm here to tell you that this is the fast track to failure.

Let's look at McDonald's as an example. Do they have the dreamiest color combo in the world? I would say no. A clown dressed in red and yellow is not my idea of cute. Did having garish brand colors hold them back from success? No, of course not. They had something way more important: a product that solved a problem for their customers. They made it reliable and convenient. And then they took over the world.

This brings me to a hard truth: if you can't sell your product without fancy branding, you won't sell it *with* fancy branding. Things like custom websites, bespoke logos, and expensive design packages only serve one purpose: they amplify and strengthen your core brand identity.

The problem comes when people try to add on these fancy extras without spending the time to lay a solid brand foundation. What happens then? Your business tends to collapse. People may like your brand for being pretty, but nobody pays you for being pretty. So run far, far away from anyone who says that they can solve your sales problem with better design.

Monetization only comes when you solve a problem. Regardless of your niche, you are in the business of solving problems. The bigger the problem you solve, the more you can charge for the solution.

If you're just starting or you're having trouble gaining traction for your brand, take a hard look at your messaging. Are you solving a problem and offering a transformational solution? If not, focus on that and that alone. The money will follow.

What is your biggest day-to-day struggle in running your business?

Without a doubt, my biggest struggle running my business day-to-day has been childcare. Can I get an amen from all the moms out there? I honestly think this is one of the biggest secrets nobody tells you before you have kids. Striking the perfect balance between work and family is impossible because the balance is constantly shifting.

Whether you work for yourself or for a more traditional job, finding quality, reliable childcare that you feel good about is not easy. Don't even get me started on the difficulties of summer, Christmas break, sick days, maternity leave, and all the many times your kids in different schools have different days off. And those were in good years! COVID-19 took this issue to a previously unimaginable level.

If you already have children of your own and do any form of work, you are probably already nodding your head. The struggle is both real and universal. I would be lying if I said that juggling family and work priorities never gets the best of me. It does from time to time. If you feel that way too, I think it's important to give yourself some grace.

When I feel overwhelmed by juggling kids and work, I always come back to one thought: Will the task at hand matter when I drop my son off for his freshman year of college? That one question is my North Star. If the answer is yes, then the task needs to be prioritized. If the answer is no, then it can probably wait a week or two without any huge consequences.

That might strike you as an odd North Star, but for me, it's powerful. I can picture the four of us standing on a sidewalk handing my son his pillow and extra-long sheets. As I hug him goodbye, I want to know that I gave my very best to the job of being his mom. I want to feel like I packed a lot of real living into those eighteen years.

I want that not just for me. I want that for him too. I want him to remember me as a mom who inspired him to chase his dreams as he watched me chase mine, but I also want him to remember me as a mom who always made time for him. (I certainly want this for both of my children. I use my son as the example here because he will be the first one to fly the nest.)

My North Star might not resonate with you, but I encourage you to identify your own North Star in your business. Navigating your way out of confusion, struggles, and frustration is so much smoother when you have a clear and tangible North Star guiding you. Without a clear destination in mind, how will you ever know if you're staying on track in your life or business?

What is the most worthwhile investment you have made for your business?

I think that worthwhile investing really comes down to your mindset. No matter what you buy, there is something to be learned and value to be gained. That said, I have found some things to be more worthwhile than others. If I had to choose just one thing, I would say that my paid networking groups have been the most valuable for me.

Building a business is something that takes time and perseverance. As soon as you put out one fire, another one pops up in a different spot. Surrounding yourself with people who understand the journey you are on is invaluable. Their support can often be the difference between reaching your goals and giving up. You can also save yourself tons of time and money learning from the experiences of others rather than always relying on trial and error.

To get the most out of these groups, you have to come from a place of service. If you invest the effort and time it takes to build genuine relationships, you have no idea what cool opportunities and fulfilling friendships will develop over the years. Want proof? My participation in this book directly results from a relationship I made in a paid membership for female entrepreneurs.

I believe in this so much that I included tips and tricks for effective networking in my signature course. Getting your brand out into the world and scaling it is a heavy lift when you're working alone. It's also an expensive process when you rely solely on paid traffic. I believe that learning to make the most of relationships will give you the best long-term return on your time and money investment.

And if you think that you could make these relationships in a free group, that's true. I just find that people tend to be a bit more invested when it's a paid group. Also, everyone has made a commitment to being there, so it's more likely that you'll get consistent engagement and follow-through.

I also want to mention that any time you invest in your business, you should go out of your way to be the kind of client or customer you want to see in your own business. Be the energy you want to attract. It sounds simple, but it's powerful.

If you lost everything today, what would you do for the next thirty days to generate income?

Let's start with some tough love. You have no business working for yourself if you can't go thirty days without income. If you rely on your business to pay bills and don't have at least three to six months of living expenses saved, rectifying that should be a top priority for you.

Look at the events of 2020. Nobody could have predicted what was coming. Of course, you can't ever be fully prepared for events on the scale of pandemics, but you should have a safety net that allows you time to pivot and adjust.

I also give this advice, having lived through the experience of losing a business. Back in 2015, I joined my first mastermind and got serious about scaling my business. I didn't know it at the time, but life had other plans for me.

My daughter was born in 2016. She is doing great now, but we almost lost her during her first year. I poured everything I had into keeping her alive. The stress was overwhelming between trips to the ER, surgeries, physical therapy, eating therapy, and various specialists. My hair was falling out of my head in clumps. It was a time of aggressive prioritization. I couldn't maintain my business on top of everything else, so I let it go.

Once she was better, I chose never to pick that exact business back up. Everything associated with that era of my life just felt too painful. I wanted a fresh start.

Assuming you don't feel quite as traumatized by your business and would like to revive it after a setback, here are some of my best tips and strategies for quick cash injections:

1. Create the VIP version of what you are already selling. I think it would be fair to say that most people struggle with implementation. We like the idea of getting in shape, but getting to the gym five days a week is another story. This same tendency can be applied to virtually every area of life. The good news is that this creates an easy way to upsell current clients. What's the VIP version of your current offering? It's simply the same offer with personalized support. This is generally an effective way to get high-quality testimonials too. The more support your client has, the better the chances of her seeing awesome results. Those awesome results then equal an awesome testimonial. That's an extra win-win. This should go without saying, but anything personalized

or DFY (done for you) should be marketed as a high-ticket offer. Don't give away your time like it's a low-ticket offer.

2. Rely on your network. When growing your business, you should always be planting seeds of friendship and genuine connection. That's the most authentic way to build a brand, and it's also something you can rely on in hard times. If you're struggling, reach out to someone you have worked with previously. That friend might be totally happy to help you out by doing a collaboration or joint promotion to their audience. Don't forget: you can only reap what you have sown. Make it a point to schedule thirty minutes each week to foster connections with other entrepreneurs. When you genuinely try to be of service to others, that goodwill will come back to you in ways you never thought possible.
3. Diversify. While this isn't explicitly a cash injection tactic, I would be remiss if I didn't mention it. You will often hear that the average millionaire has seven streams of income. I have never been able to find an actual study that substantiates this number, but I know from experience that the heart of that idea is true. My husband and I got into real estate investing for this reason. Is reading all one hundred pages of Texas property law a thrilling way to spend an afternoon? Not really. But is it unlikely that all of your streams of income will collapse at the same time? Historically speaking, yes. When trying to ensure income stability in your business, the best defense is a good offense.

How can people connect with you?

I can be found at bonjourbranding.com and on Instagram @bonjour.branding.

AS YOU START SHARING WHAT YOU KNOW, YOU'LL FIND THAT PEOPLE ADMIRE YOU FOR KNOWING HOW TO DO THAT LITTLE SOMETHING YOU THOUGHT EVERYONE KNEW HOW TO DO.

Sarah Lawyer

CHAPTER 14

EXPANDING YOUR REACH BY SARAH LAWYER

I started my entrepreneurial journey like many entrepreneurs: in network marketing. I fell in love with the business model. I started my own business without any overhead, without needing to have my own products. At first, I was able to get nominal results. I recruited many new members through my family. Then it stalled, and nothing changed for five more years. I bought many different courses, I joined a few different masterminds, but I never found my "thing" that could bring me success. I was just about to give up! I thought maybe this entrepreneurial journey wasn't for me, that maybe I'm not supposed to be able to work from home and change my family's life.

I was at my lowest point. That was when I was introduced to Pinterest for business. I thought, Pinterest for business? Is that even possible? I *love* Pinterest. I was on there at least a couple of times a week looking for recipes, looking for my next new hairstyle, for my next home idea; I never thought I could find success in building my business on Pinterest. Boy, was I wrong! As soon as I made my personal account into a business account and started putting my business products out there, I began to make sales. I started to get leads. All without using advertising!

This was the start of something new and exciting for me. I started helping other entrepreneurs realize the incredible power behind Pinterest as a business. So I did a complete pivot in my own business. I'm still part of the network marketing community because from my time in that area, I learned the basics of running a business. Those basics are communication, marketing, and how to nurture current customers. Now instead of focusing entirely on that, I focus on my own business that includes helping fellow mom entrepreneurs—or as I like to call us, MomPreneurs—build and develop their business by finding their passion and expanding their reach and influence into the world by using the search power of Pinterest.

What is your *why* or purpose for your business?

I briefly mentioned in my introduction what I do, but now I want to share with you *why* and the purpose behind what I do.

I have always felt a calling to make a difference in the world, and when I graduated college, I felt the world telling me that the only way I could make a difference was to become a mother. Being a mother *is* an amazing blessing! I wouldn't trade anything in the world for my beautiful daughters who bring so much joy to my life. But I also felt a pull and a calling to give something more to the world. It took me quite a few years to figure out how, and I don't think I have even scratched the surface of my potential. I do what I do to help other moms put their vision of their business into the world and then be found in a peaceful, organic way.

Motherhood is a very challenging place to build a business. Work times can be unplanned and chaotic. They are often very early or very late. And they are usually minimal. So I want to show them an easier way to be found without spending hours every day on social media. For years, that's what I did. I posted daily, I showed up in stories, I messaged cold prospects, I messaged warm prospects, and it was exhausting. But as soon as I turned my attention into building my business on Pinterest, I started seeing results. And that's what I want to give my stressed-out mothers: another way to build their business that allows people to find them instead of always searching and asking for attention through the usual routes of Facebook or Instagram.

What are the biggest mistakes you see new entrepreneurs making?

Not having their own website. Here's an interesting bit for you to consider as I explain how you can utilize what's available to build your business. There are three top search engines:

1. Google,
2. YouTube, and
3. Pinterest.

Many entrepreneurs fail to include them in their business strategy. They are search engines, which means you're not interrupting them on social media to say, "Take a look at my business." People are already searching for your business, and just to prove it, I'm going to give you examples of three different business types—brick and mortar, service-based, and product-based—and how to play the long game of building your business:

1. Brick-and-mortar business: I see many great businesses get started without a website. For this example, I'm going to use a dog-grooming service. One big mistake I've seen is that when I go to Google and search for the business, I'm taken to a Facebook page. This can be a great place to start, but not to host it full-time. What happens to your business if Facebook completely shuts down? Are your customers going to find you? Contact you? Pay for the product or service that you offer at your store? If you have a website, you have more opportunities to attract the customer to your business. Another reason I wanted to point out the

importance of a website is to share your content. Since space you "rent" on Facebook is not technically your own, they can take down your content if they feel it isn't right for the space. You don't have to worry about that on a website. You'll want to make sure that you have all your disclaimers ready for the legality, but you own that space. You can start by sharing tips about your business. Share it in a video or a blog post, or offer those tips as a lead magnet. Build an email list offering a valuable source of information, like how to choose the best shears to groom your dog. The person who downloads this will continue to get your tips around dog grooming (hint: continue to send them emails providing tips). You may be asking, why give away all my secrets? By sharing your secrets and tips, they get to know, like, and trust you, and when they don't want to groom their dog, they will give you a call and book your service. Before we go on to the next business, I want to share how you can use this for Pinterest (my favorite).

When putting your business up on Pinterest, I want you to remember how people use the top three search engines I mentioned above. When I'm looking for a dog groomer, I use Google; when I'm looking for how to do dog grooming, I use YouTube; when I'm looking for how to do the dog grooming and ideas for future use, I use Pinterest. For example, I may feel excited to attempt dyeing my dog's fur, so I'm going to look for pictures of other dogs that have been groomed how I like it. Pinterest ties YouTube and Google together. People go to Pinterest to look for ideas, to plan out what they will do. So feature your dog-grooming clients on Pinterest for people to pin as a future idea. The funny thing is that those pins will end up being searched on Google.

Now, creating a website doesn't have to be very fancy or complex. You can create a simple website using Squarespace, Shopify, Wix, Etsy, and more, and all of these will allow me (your potential customer) to pay you and book your services or buy your products.

2. Service-based business: Let's talk about applying this for a service, like a coaching business that helps people develop their digital products or services. You decide to start right, so you create your website and have a valuable lesson attracting your ideal client. You have a way for people to download a three-to-five-page PDF or watch a five-to-ten-minute video sharing this valuable lesson once they enter their name and email. You have a campaign set up to nurture these leads for a few days so they learn to know, like, and trust your business. The next step is for you to start sharing tips that are the simplified version of what they get when they become clients.

   You can share these tips in writing form through a blog post or in a YouTube video, or both. I have a client who records a YouTube video once a week and then transcribes it into written form as a blog post. Now her potential customer can find her on YouTube and Google; if she has her website, she can share this information on Pinterest too. The mistake that this business may be making is not creating the content that their potential client is looking for on Google, YouTube, and Pinterest. To make sure you don't fall into this trap, do some keyword research. In this chapter, I go into further detail on how to do the keyword research. Pinterest has created a way for clients to find them, engage in their content, and buy from them. Always make sure your call to action in the content you're writing/recording refers them to your capture page or sales page to subscribe to your service to become your next coaching client.

3. Products-based business: For this business, we're going to use a makeup company. Start with a website so you have a way to capture emails and communicate with potential buyers via an email service. Continue to provide value and tips on using makeup. Post pictures of your product on Pinterest. This may seem like an oversimplified answer, but it's a mistake I've seen. They post the photos on the product page of their website but forget to share those exact images to Pinterest. Pinterest is a shopper's platform. Your customers go there looking for their next eyeshadow, lipstick, and foundation that will make them feel fabulous and confident. Also, make sure to call out your potential customers: busy moms, high school kids looking for makeup for prom, and soon-to-be brides looking for their next fancy makeup tutorial. To point them out, use the images they will relate to, use their language, and use their search terms. By doing this, you are now going to show up more frequently in the search results. This requires you to narrow down your client avatar and understand their struggles and pain.

Which activities do you perform that generate the majority of your revenue?

I have spoken about the many ways you can generate revenue through search optimization, and I share them because they have generated the majority of my revenue.

When I went through the masterminds and coaching programs, I was always directed to build my business using Facebook. There is no doubt that Facebook is and can be a cash machine. However, it wasn't for me, and it isn't for many other entrepreneurs I know. That's why I'm writing this. I want to give you another option. The majority of my revenue comes from blogging about products I enjoy and then leading people to the buy button.

Another way that has created revenue for me has been through interviews. Don't be the next best-kept secret. You have to share your brilliance. Find people who host podcasts on the topic that is your genius and reach out to them. See if they're looking for someone to interview. You never know until you ask.

Allow people to find you. Put yourself out there on Google by sharing what people are searching for, putting your business tips on Pinterest, recording a video tip, and placing it on YouTube. Be found! Don't let your genius go unheard. Social media is a powerful thing if you can consistently show up day in and day out. As a mom, consistency is tied up around my kids. So change your thinking from getting people's attention on social media to being found in search engines. For me, it takes a lot less time to create a weekly piece or even a biweekly piece of content than shows up daily on social media.

As part of being found, you want to start sharing what people are searching for. I can just feel you asking the question, How do you find that? How do you know what to share? Here's a list of tools I recommend:

- Google,
- Pinterest,
- YouTube,
- AnswerThePublic.com, and
- UberSuggest.com.

The last two, Answerthepublic.com and Ubersuggest.com, simply plug in your topic of choice. You'll be presented with what people are searching for on that topic or similar search terms and how often they are searched within thirty days.

The top three search engines, Google, Pinterest, and YouTube, are a little more complex to explain. When you pull up the search bar in any of these, start typing and, before you hit enter, stop! You'll notice a drop-down of other options to search. These are what people are searching, what they've searched for in the past, and what is being suggested to the current searcher around the topic. These top three search engines want to give you up-to-date information while searching. As the business owner, you can use these options to know what people are searching for and provide content around these search terms.

Just like that, you now have content that shows up in search results. Now it's up to you to provide what people want. You'll be amazed at how quickly people start buying from your site because you've given them what they were searching for.

What is one of your greatest failures that ultimately led to success?

Relying on products and services from network marketing companies instead of realizing I have so much to offer the world. When I finally decided to step out of the shadows of my network marketing company, I was terrified. What did I know about making money since I had made all of seven hundred dollars in four years of striving to build a network marketing business? But once I decided to become my own business founder, CEO of MomPreneur Initiative, everything changed. I finally sold my services and I sold my products. And the interesting thing was, the more I shared about what I have learned regarding building my business and my expertise, the more my network marketing customer base grew.

I finally realized why some network marketing professionals are so successful and others like myself were not. The difference between the top producers and myself was that I relied solely on what the network marketing company provided for influence. I never put my expertise out into the marketplace. I used to think that I didn't have anything to offer. If you've ever felt this way, understand you have the expertise and have something valuable that no one else can give to people. You are unique. You see the world differently than anyone else out there. I want you to start sharing it. As you start sharing what you know, you'll find that people admire you for knowing how to do that little something you thought everyone knew how to do.

My biggest mistake was not sharing what tasks I've learned to do that I assumed everyone knew how to do. This little secret has led to my success because I have shared my genius and have allowed others to see what I can do for them. I help people create images that speak to what they are offering. I help MomPreneurs develop a business plan to make an impact. And I can help you be discovered and found using Pinterest.

What is your biggest day-to-day struggle in running your business?

Time! As a MomPreneur, time is my biggest struggle, which is why learning to use what you have correctly is so vital. For this, I have four big tips:

1. Learn how to batch. The idea of batching is to get everything around a certain task done in one day. For example, my batching looks like this: Mondays/Tuesdays are clients' days. Wednesdays are writing days, which include blog posts, emails, sales pages, posts. Thursday is recording day or the second writing day, depending on the projects I'm currently working on. If it's a recording day, I plan to have my hair and makeup done to record a video. Fridays are learning days. As an entrepreneur, you should always be learning. This is different from reading a self-development book. This is diving into courses or listening to an event recording that will help you apply a new technique to push your business forward.
2. Use a planner. It can be physical or digital, but it needs to be out of your head. Have you ever felt overwhelmed and anxious about all the things you need to do from day to day? I know I have, and I've come to realize that the days I feel like this are the days I haven't written out my priorities.

I haven't scheduled out my tasks. I've left everything in my head. Your brain is the most amazing tool out there, but it can only handle so much. Give yourself an edge on your work time every day by taking all the "need to dos" out of your mind so you can focus on what needs to be done.

3. Automate your activities. The last bit of advice I would give is to find a way to automate your business. For example, building your business on Pinterest can be done in just a few hours per month through automation tools. Emails can be sent out by using automation. Instagram and Facebook posts can be scheduled to go out every day. When you find ways to automate your business, you can take yourself out of the day-to-day tasks and focus on the meat of your business. The meat is making the sale, creating content, running webinars, being interviewed, teaching from stage. These are the activities that generate the most income in your business.
4. Delegate tasks. The last part is delegating and hiring someone else to help you with small tasks. I've been taught this by a few different coaches in my life: your time is valuable. Time is the only thing you cannot buy more of. You can't ever get it back. So do you need to be spending time mowing the lawn, doing the laundry, cleaning up the dishes, running your social media sites, editing the videos? Or can some of these tasks be delegated or hired out at a nominal rate? Let me ask you this: How much is your time worth right now? First, add up your monthly income. Next, add up how much time you spend working to get that income. When you divide your income by your hours, are you making as much as you thought you were? Do some of these tasks not seem as important now when you can hire a neighbor kid to mow the lawn for you? Or a college student to help schedule out your posts? There may be certain tasks

that require a professional and are a larger expense. Save up and find that person when you can afford it.

If you lost everything today, what would you do for the next thirty days to generate income?

First, I would create a list of my skills in great detail, from knowing how to create an image and writing a blog or social media post. Everything would need to go on my list. Then I would rate each skill by how much I enjoy doing it. The top three would be my focus to set myself up on Upwork or Fiverr as someone to hire for these skills. By doing this, I start to build up a customer base. The next step would be to create a free website and, if I have enough money, claim a domain URL for this website. Finally, I would offer a lead magnet based on my services that people loved. Use those testimonials from my work on Upwork or Fiverr and add them to a sales page where I sell these services for more revenue.

I would let people know what I'm doing and how to find me. It may start with Facebook or Instagram to get attention. A two-week posting schedule around one main topic and posting every day to build some momentum. While setting up my website, I start sharing my aha moments from working with those who hired me. By doing this, people will have seen what I'm doing, my business will start ranking on search engines (because I did my research on what people are searching for), and I will have a head start to building my email list.

How can people connect with you?

I can be found at sarahlawyer.com and on Instagram @sarahmompreneur.

LIVING A SUCCESSFUL LIFE MEANS ALSO ACHIEVING SUCCESS IN THE AREAS OF YOUR LIFE THAT MAKE LIFE WORTH LIVING.

Christy Mayfield

CHAPTER 15

LIVING YOUR DREAM BY CHRISTY MAYFIELD

I'm the Founder and CEO of Christy Mayfield Coaching LLC. I help high-achieving professional women worldwide grow and scale their businesses, while simultaneously enhancing their relationships, and their emotional and physical health, using my signature system that focuses on the three core pillars to a wildly successful life. I held a prestigious, lucrative medical career for nearly thirty years, yet I was burned out working sixty to seventy hours a week, exhausted and missing out on life with family and friends.

I started working as a certified physician assistant straight out of college and have spent nearly thirty years providing medical care to patients in emergency medicine, women's health, and family medicine. I was passionate about being emotionally present for others during some of their most challenging, as well as exciting, times. The experience of sharing the depths of someone's innermost feelings is a sacred place to be.

Let me ask you a question. Despite feeling passionate about your work, do you ever feel like you are being pulled in a thousand different directions and not having much to show for it? You know, feeling like you're not satisfied? Feeling like there's a piece missing, that if you could figure out what it was, everything would finally come together? I get it. I've been there!

Working in a level one trauma center in one of the largest emergency departments in the nation, had me pulled in a thousand different directions at once, without much time to catch my breath in between. In addition, I was supervising about thirty staff in the emergency department, running a household, writing a book, and trying to care for my own physical and emotional needs, which, I'm sure just like you, got pushed to the bottom of my list of priorities. I was at the peak of my career, but the other areas of my life that were equally important to me were suffering for it.

Living a successful life means also achieving success in the areas of your life that make life worth living. This means having the ability to be fully present for your children when they need you, having time to connect with your partner, having space in your day to do the things that both energize you or allow for rest, as you need it.

Wouldn't it be nice to have time to exercise if you felt like it or just take a nap on the couch if you were tired? Or how about this: having the time to travel to the destinations that are calling your heart? More importantly, I'm talking about the joy that comes from these special times and the memories you create from the experiences. The experiences that you're probably missing out on right now. I want you to be able to sit in your rocking chair when you're ninety years old on the front porch, looking out at the world, knowing you have lived a successful life, not just a successful business. You know what I mean, right?

It took one dying patient in the emergency department who cracked something wide open in me that flooded my whole being with an aha moment. I realized I didn't go into medicine to save people's physical lives. That dying man opened me to the knowledge that I went into medicine because I wanted to hold that sacred space for someone as they confronted the challenges and emotions that life brings. I tried to use my ability to guide someone toward wholeness—body, mind, and soul—as they faced the perceived obstacles that life throws.

I wanted to help them as they navigated their way through the transitions that life presents us with and help them find peace. To feel hope and discover what the future holds, they knew the next best steps to elevate their lives, and that's why I spent five more years training as a transformational coach. I learned various coaching modalities to help elevate your business, relationships, and mental and physical health and to ultimately live your wildly successful life.

I utilize my signature coaching system to help six- and seven-figure female entrepreneurs and professional women scale their businesses and their careers while simultaneously elevating their personal relationships and enhancing their physical and mental health. This is without sacrificing one for the other so they can live a wildly successful life, free from burnout! That's where my concept of the three pillars of success comes from. Mind, body, and soul translated into real daily life represents our business, our own mental and physical well-being, and our relationships. It's also important to note that in my thirty years practicing medicine, I have seen, and science has proven, that many illnesses and diseases results from chronic stress. Simply put, stress is how we perceive the events around us. Therefore, stress is a result of our thoughts and emotions. It's a perception created in our mind that generates a tangible or physical outcome.

We are often blocking our success, but we're also the only person we can control, so our power is 100 percent in our hands to create the results we want to achieve. Thus, Christy Mayfield Coaching was founded.

What is your *why* or purpose for your business?

I coach female entrepreneurs and professional women to uplevel themselves as thought leaders in their industries without burnout so they can live the lifestyle they desire *now*, not someday down the road. We create our business to live a particular lifestyle. Still, too many times, I see women on the struggle bus, scaling their businesses at the expense of their relationships and their own mental and physical health. It doesn't have to be that way.

Doing this limits you to only achieving one-third of the success you're capable of creating. You can have it all when you understand the three core pillars of success and how to pull them together in a cohesive, peaceful way so you can be wildly successful in your business, connected more fully to the people you love who are most important to you, and have the mental and physical energy to enjoy the life you've created.

I've been implementing my techniques in my life for years and the lives of my clients so they can enjoy the relationships with their partners, their children, family, and friends. So they have time to take the trips to the destinations that are calling their hearts. It's the memories we make along the way, not at the end.

There is no "end" when we're growing a business, and you don't want to look back fifty years down the road and see you built an empire, but you missed out on the joy of living it with the people you love. That's how we experience the joy that our business success has provided us. That's how we become wildly successful not just in business but in life.

This inspired me to pull together all my knowledge and training to create a scientifically proven system based on neuroscience for transforming all the pieces in your life that you're currently juggling into a peaceful, cohesive system that will uplevel your career, your relationships, and your well-being so you really *can* have it all!

What are the biggest mistakes you see new entrepreneurs making?

The biggest mistakes and missteps I see small business owners making are:

1. Doing "all the things."

   When I started Christy Mayfield Coaching LLC, I was doing "all the things." You know what I mean, the new and best ideas touted by every guru? And as soon as I finished one, such as a course or a new marketing funnel, I barely got it up and running when a new trend was touted in place of the widely popular one the week before. Metaphorically, I felt like I was running back and forth across the basketball court when I was in middle school PE class . . . and I hated it. As soon as I felt like I reached the spot that everyone told me I was supposed to be, I'd look over my shoulder. Everyone was running in the opposite direction again toward another new fad in the marketing arena. All I did was run myself ragged until I was exhausted, trying to do what everyone said I should be doing until it was no longer fun. I was exhausted, and I had little to show for it.

   What's worse, as I struggled to do all the things everyone else said I should be doing, I became further and further disconnected from myself, my unique gifts and talents, and my passion, which was limiting my success!

2. Forgetting to invest in yourself. *You* are the biggest asset in your business.

   I was single, juggling my day job, working until 1:30 or even three in the morning, creating funnels, copywriting scripts, writing email nurtures, and trying to balance my relationships with my friends and family. As a result, I often felt like I had no time to answer the phone or return calls, my dating life was nonexistent, I stopped making time for exercise, and I gained weight.

   No amount of money that you invest in your business will get you to your goals if you don't also invest in yourself, because *you* are the glue that holds your business together—not the funnels, not the automation, not all the copywriting in the world. You are the biggest investment in your business!

I know the struggle of juggling career and life, trying to stay focused on your work without feeling guilt in your personal life, getting traction in your business, only to lose momentum when you make time to have lunch with your friends. Despite all the family time I missed out on and the invitations I declined, I still wasn't where I wanted to be. I was overwhelmed and felt defeated, even though I knew what I had to offer was valuable. Instead of giving up that day, I had an epiphany. I decided to take a different approach to my business.

Before I prioritized myself in my business and invested in myself as much as I invested in courses, additional training, webinars, and all the other shiny objects along the way, I was burned out and discouraged and attempted to follow everyone else's path. I continued to follow the business gurus, doing everything they said I should be doing. I lost my motivation. I was plagued by headaches, body aches, and it wasn't long before a feeling of hopelessness set in. I began to doubt myself, wondering if my dream would ever truly materialize.

I hit the pause button and turned inward. I discovered the techniques that allowed me to ultimately stop playing small, let go of perfectionism (which was a death grip on my dreams), and got out of my own way.

3. Holding on to attachment.

Letting go of the attachments, the expectations I had, for a specific outcome in my business was crucial to opening the door for the right opportunities to flow in. It allowed me to become more resilient, alleviate any business anxiety, and slay my emotional triggers.

4. Not being intentional about the choices you make.

   Often, we let our past experiences dictate the choices we make for our future. Instead, I became intentional with the decisions I made. This means, when I made a decision, I ensured it was in alignment with the future I wanted to create and not based on old, automatic patterns from the past that no longer served me for the place I was in my life. Remember, it's about upleveling! This allowed me to enhance my business and my personal life in a way that created balance and peace so I was able to succeed at both.

   Eliminating these four mistakes changed everything for me, and I now work with my clients to achieve the same success! When I was able to get clear on my deepest desires, hear my inner voice, eliminate the emotional and mental blocks that were subconsciously holding me back, knowing how to make the right decisions to prevent me from spending years heading down the wrong path, and creating an action plan for reaching my short-term and ultimately long-term goals, I was able to reduce my stress and enhance my motivation, my creativity, my productivity, and my profits. That's when business and financial opportunities began flowing toward me. After that, things started to feel effortless.

What is one of your greatest failures that ultimately led to success?

At the beginning of my career, I had many limiting beliefs and emotional blocks around money, success, sales, and imposter syndrome, to name a few. When I was able to recognize and resolve my limiting beliefs, as they came up, as well as the emotional blocks that were holding me back, my success in my business, as well as my dating life, skyrocketed. (It's true—how you show up in one area of your life is how you show up in other areas of your life!) It took having my coach recognize what I could not see in myself because I was too close to see it.

Today, I always know when I'm hitting up against another subconscious limiting belief or an emotional block, because invariably my success begins to plateau. Once I coach myself through it, I can jump-start my success every time. From my experience, over the years as a transformational coach, I have developed, tested, redeveloped, and launched some pretty amazing things for thousands of women to help them achieve the same success in their businesses, personal relationships, and life by resolving their limiting beliefs and emotional blocks. These are the things preventing them from reaching the success they are capable of! Investing in myself and doing my coaching allowed me to skyrocket my opportunities.

What hard lessons have you learned that could have been avoided?

So many of my clients come to me after having spent years heading down the wrong path. Knowing your deepest subconscious desires for your life and business early on will prevent years of lost time heading down the wrong path doing what you *think* you should do or what other people think you should do, or what all the latest gurus are telling you to do.

One of the first things my clients and I do together is uncover their subconscious desires for every part of their life that is important to them. Even the parts they didn't know were important to them. This saves years heading down the wrong path, only to discover too late that you weren't making the choices that were in alignment with your deepest dreams and goals. Of course, we all have to pivot now and then in business, but pivoting along the right path is far easier than making a huge U-turn after you've driven one thousand miles in the wrong direction.

Once that's accomplished, they stop wasting time making the wrong choices. Instead, they begin making the right choices that align with their deepest subconscious desires, connected to their greatest gifts and unique talents. I call it the "spillover theory" for good or for bad. When I did that, my visibility skyrocketed and the opportunities began pouring in, not only for my business but my personal life as well. I go into the spillover theory below.

What have you found helps with blending your personal and professional life?

There are three core pillars to having a successful life: our purpose/career, our own physical and mental health, and the relationships we have in our lives that nurture us. When one of these core pillars is compromised, the other two core pillars will automatically become compromised, leading to a perpetual jog on the hamster wheel. You'll try to keep up and feel like you're not really living, just existing. I call this the "spillover theory."

When our businesses are depleting the other important areas of our lives, we're not living our dream life, no matter how successful our businesses become. Remember the times you've heard about some of the wealthiest people not being happy? Despite their business and financial success, they're still left feeling empty, seeking something that's missing. What's often missing is the other two pillars necessary for living a wildly successful life! All the business success and all the money in the world will never create a dream lifestyle if you've sacrificed your relationships and your health to achieve it.

You won't achieve success without knowing how to elevate each of the three core pillars in your life and maintain that elevated state. Women have the ability to not only balance their career, relationships, and personal well-being, but they have the ability to enhance each of those areas in a cohesive, exciting, peaceful way that can last a lifetime.

Make choices that align with your deepest subconscious desires of business, relationships, and your own mental and physical health. For example, my clients who work with me for one-on-one coaching can achieve their short-term goals in each of the three core pillars over six months of working together, and many choose to continue working with me as they continue to uplevel their business, their relationships, and their health. The first step when we work together is taking an inventory of the three core pillars of their life. Next, we access their deepest subconscious desires for their life.

What comes up is individualized to each person. Really exciting insight is made during these sessions and serves to guide each client's path forward. The client chooses what they want to achieve in each area, and we spend the next six months working to achieve those goals. They have found my coaching to be important to their success. Together, we can identify the limiting beliefs and emotional blocks preventing their success and disrupting the blending of their personal and professional lives.

They make choices based on the deepest desires in their hearts, the messages their emotions are providing, and know how to determine if each choice that presents itself and each decision they make is in alignment with the life they are trying to create. And even more exciting, because my coaching is based on neuroscience, my clients' changes stay as long as they continue using the coaching techniques they learn. This allows them to maintain that cohesive enhanced blend of the three core pillars necessary for success in both their personal and professional lives without compromising one for the other.

What self-care, routines, and habits do you have to maintain good health?

I do my daily self-coaching, often using my process of ebb and flow. This process guides my decision-making to ensure that my choices will lead me toward those dreams and goals I have for my present and my future, rather than further away. It also helps to alleviate anxiety or overwhelm on the spot. In summary, it looks like this:

- E: identify the **Emotion**
- B: connect with the **Body**
- F: **Find** the thought
- L: **Listen** to your heart
- OW: **Observe** the **Wisdom**

Our emotions are here to serve us, not torment us. They have messages for us and are there to guide us. You may be asking how. It's simple: our thoughts create our emotions, and our emotions drive our actions. So, to be successful in business and relationships and life, you have to first know how to listen to your emotions' messages, because your emotions ultimately drive the actions you take, leading you toward or away from your success.

What is the most worthwhile investment you have made for your business?

Investing in myself and hiring my coach. A coach can see from a perspective that you are unable to see because you're too close to it. A coach can keep you accountable and guide you through the next steps to achieve the wildly successful life that you seek. You can't break through the glass ceiling without a trained coach who has been there, done that, and is committed to walking with you through your own uniquely fabulous journey.

My coach guided me in peeling back more and more layers that I would never have discovered independently. Without the guidance from my coach, so many of the gifts and talents that I was meant to bring to this world would have remained locked inside.

If you lost everything today, what would you do for the next thirty days to generate income?

Networking with like-minded, high-achieving women. I truly believe that we become who we surround ourselves with. When you connect with a networking community of like-minded, high-achieving women, who are one step ahead of where you are, you will continue to move the dial in your business forward. The referral opportunities abound! Speaking opportunities will present themselves, and you will continue to gain visibility and new clients.

The aspirations you have for your career and your life will only be as strong, successful, sustainable, and scalable as you are. If your mental and physical health becomes compromised, your business will also become compromised. When you invest in caring for yourself, it is equivalent to caring for your business.

How can people connect with you?

I can be found at christymayfield.com.

WHEN YOU LEAD WITH YOUR HEART AND SOUL, YOU SIMPLY CANNOT GET IT WRONG.

Amanda Monnier

CHAPTER 16

SOUL ALIGNMENT AND CONSCIOUS CREATION BY AMANDA MONNIER

I am a former probation officer turned energy healer and mindset coach—you definitely do not hear of career pivots like that regularly. I lived and breathed in my masculine energy. It was how I kept myself safe for many years. I held myself to levels of perfection that were nearly unattainable and found that I was always in constant action mode, later resulting in complete burnout. I was my own worst critic and hid from everything that was authentically me. This is reflected in my body, skin, and overall view of life. I was tired and riddled with acne and damn near forgot who I was at a deeper level. Which is what I have come to understand as the real reason we are here in the first place.

I lived in a world where I was more focused on all the things that others thought I should do or told me to do, and I was fucking terrified of getting in trouble. Ultimately, I realized in my late twenties that I was living my life on the terms and rules of other people. I did that thing . . . you know, where we grow up too soon, lose our innocence, graduate high school, pick a college major and potential career out of some catalog, do the college thing, and jump into the workforce. We reach the place of adulthood in the blink of an eye. It's like that adage many of us heard as kids: "Don't grow up too fast." We have been conditioned to see life through this clouded lens: once you hit adulthood, it all goes from fun to uninspired "workin' for the man," get that job, buy that house, find a partner, get to retirement, etc. I'm here to tell you that this is a crock of shit. I'm telling you this because I wish someone would have told me this as a little girl. So here it goes . . .

Wisdom Drop #1—If you're living in a world where the things that take the majority of your time and energy are *not* things that light you up and inspire you, there is a problem on all levels (mind, body, soul).

I've had so many amazing opportunities in my life and, do not get me wrong, I'm entirely grateful. I would not be who I am today without these experiences, and I would not be helping other women shift out of the places that I once was. The bigger picture and point here is that rapid soul expansion and our ability to go from uninspired autopilot to soul-aligned bliss are available at *any* moment. Yes, it is a process, but it is also a remembrance—a remembrance of who you truly are at a soul level and the brilliance you came here to unleash to the planet. You get to feel good and be aligned in what you spend most of your life doing (if you choose it—some people never do).

This used to be me. How did we get to the place where the majority of humans spend their time at a place (aka work) they do not absolutely love? If you do not believe in your ability to design a soul-aligned dream life that you love waking up to every day, borrow my certainty that it is possible and *will* happen once you begin to understand a few basic things (which I'll get into in a moment).

In my old life (the eight-to-five grind, as I like to call it), I woke up feeling uninspired as hell and intuitively knew there was a bigger purpose for my life. I had this feeling since I was a little girl. I just did not yet understand it at a conscious level. I knew I was meant to show up in a massive way and impact women around the world. I quit my career in law enforcement and the placeholder job

I shifted into for several months after that, gave up my pension and health care, sold my home, and moved to a new city. This was a bit terrifying at first, so if you're in this space at the moment, I get you entirely. I have been there.

Within six months of the initial leap of going all in, I started a business, this business, as it was (and is) fully in alignment with all of me. I was divinely guided along the way—*that* is for damn sure. The universe and my higher self never steered me wrong once I went all in and said yes to the uncomfortable shift that led to magic in my life! I can say I will never *not* do this on my terms, I will never again ask permission for another meal break, coffee break, day/holiday off, do daily tasks that hurt my soul, or do menial shit just to check boxes and collect a paycheck.

Wisdom Drop #2—This is not just available to you. This is *your birthright.* This is a choice. This requires an identity shift (if you are not already doin' the things). This is about you embodying the next-level version of yourself. This aspect of you is soul-aligned and does shit on your terms.

What is your *why* or purpose for your business?

I am a woman on a mission to create a movement of healing, intuitively connected badass goddesses. These women have healed and broken ancestral cycles and released pain and trauma from the past. My purpose is to guide women in aligning with their heart and soul, creating a life on their terms, and passionately unleashing their gifts to the planet. We need your special sauce, like, yesterday.

We are all intuitive. It's about remembering this and learning how to use this intuition muscle. We are conditioned to look outside of ourselves for answers when, at a soul level, we already know.

The paradigm shift is happening on the planet *now*. When you lead with your heart and soul, you simply cannot get it wrong. When you are taking inspired action based on the things that light you up, there is no way you can fail. You are your kind of special sauce—unique and weird in your own way. I love weird, by the way! This is what you harness and channel in your business. This lights up the freaking planet because you are lit up while doing it!

Wisdom Drop #3—That intangible thing inside of you that wants to come out is unique to your soul; every human has something inside of them to bring to life. When this passion and light are unleashed authentically, the financial outcome is secondary.

The customers and clients are also a result of this magic being released. The "thing" magnetizing your clients and any moving pieces to your business is the authenticity and soul alignment you are exuding. You are mirroring this to your peeps and reminding them of who they are to the depths of their soul by shining your unique light. I once heard a saying, and it goes something like this: "The teacher will show up when the student is ready." I believe we resonate with the people on our journey based on their energy and readiness to uplevel into our infinite potential. A heart-centered business is about building a soul community that resonates on every level. I work with my soul-mate clients (aligned clients that are ready, willing, and able to say yes to themselves and this work). It actually doesn't even feel like work most of the time!

At the end of the day, I built my business on the following vision and foundational principles I live and breathe by:

- I'm here to inspire thousands that will lead to millions in creating a life from heart and soul alignment on your damn terms.
- I will constantly remind anyone and everyone ready to hear this message: you can do what you love and unleash magic out to the planet (and you can monetize that shit).
- You can release old triggers, heal deep emotional pain, and shift what may feel like impossible amounts of trauma. There is a way, and for my clients, I do the heavy lifting in this area.
- Conscious creation is a proven method to energetically plant seeds of what you deeply desire in your physical reality. It

is scientific, and it works! What I was able to shift in just under twelve months is life-changing. If someone told me a couple of years ago I would be running the business I love on *my* terms, I would have probably laughed.

What are the biggest mistakes you see new entrepreneurs making?

Building a business that does not feel congruent or aligned with your heart and soul. This would be a business that does not light you up, a business that does not work for you and is not in your favor.

Strategy is one thing we all implement into business. It is necessary. However, I see so many people coming from needy, desperate energy—trying to find clients and talk them into working together instead of attracting them with their vibe and certainty of what they have to offer is of massive value.

The energy you put into action, or any task, will dictate the outcome. Period. If you hate sales calls and are constantly getting on the phone or dropping into someone's DMs (nothing is more of a turnoff in business than this icky energy) trying to talk people into your services and explain to them why they need you, you are pushing against the very thing you desire with your silent instructions (your disbelief that the universe is working for you when you take inspired action, the fact you do not need to force it).

Feel into the following two statements for a second:

- Energy #1: My soul-aligned clients love to pay me. They feel my energy through the output of my content. When I am in an inspired state, I put myself out there and share content of massive value from my heart. My clients find me when I am visible and in my authentic truth. They ask how they can work with me. They have been waiting for me to show up. My clients see the value I bring, and it's a fuck yes for them in working with me!

Versus

- Energy #2: I have thirty sales calls I need to make today. Maybe my virtual assistant can drop fifty DMs. I'm bound to get at least one client. Oh, shit, I have bills to pay, and what am I going to do if I don't get these sales from my launch? Maybe I'll do a live video or give something away for free. Maybe I'll follow up repeatedly with my cold leads. I have to close the month out strong.

Which energy feels better?

Which energy are you more attracted to?

Someone who is grounded and knows their worth, or the person who is in needy, desperate energy and forcing things into place?

Wisdom Drop #4—That sparkle you send out into the world will hit and magnetize the people who resonate with you on a soul level and who are ready to go for it. Know your worth. Embody your worth. Run your business from a place of heart and soul alignment. If it does not feel good (aligned), don't do it.

Feel into if it's fear holding you back from your next level or if it's that something simply is not for you. *Big* difference. This is a life-changing tidbit that will change the foundation of your business. Your business is a reflection of you and the energy you bring to it. A solid foundation of knowing who you are and what is aligned for you, along with inspired action from those heart/soul pings that light you up. This is the business special sauce, and the feminine is leading the way with this powerful business strategy.

What hard lessons have you learned that could have been avoided?

Where to start . . . If I could go back to my younger self and give her advice, it would be entirely related to shifting out of the fear of being 100 percent authentically me (which, my hope is some of you reading this can skip the years of spinning your wheels and jump right into this sweet spot, creating massive shifts without the unnecessary stuck-ness).

I hid in the spiritual closet for *years*. I played small. I shoved myself into the monotonous societal mold, and pieces of me started to die (I later found out they were pieces of my soul dying to be heard). I did this in a myriad of areas: relationship, career, family, etc.

I did not understand how the universe truly works and how to manifest the deepest desires of what was and always had been inside of me. I always felt there was a missing piece to the puzzle, and I refused to stop until I found answers. The journey is part of human life. I don't begin to deny or minimize it. If I could share one thing with my younger self in addition to just being me, even if it was messy as hell, it would be this: how to tap into my heart (which connects you with your unique soul blueprint) and create from a place of intention.

I learned a method of conscious creation (one I use daily) through a combination of intuition, certifications, courses, and training. First and foremost, you are not a broken person and you do not need to be fixed. That is one of the most fucked-up things about the personal development industry and something my mentor (Chris Duncan) drilled into my head over and over again. We are divine beings and we are here for a beautiful life full of fun.

Wisdom Drop #5—We are meant to feel good the majority of the time. The immense pain in the human condition is rooted in an identity that is simply not you. This results in forgetting who you are and blocks your channel to your inner wisdom and connection with the divine.

Getting into the results of what you desire just because you'd love to have it is the *first thing* I highly recommend if you like to shift things in your physical reality. It energetically sends a message out into the universe and plants the seeds of creation. It provides clear instructions to the universe and what you have chosen. The universe communicates in frequency (aka your feelings, thoughts, and emotions, which all comprise your identity). The mind and body do not know the difference between visualization and feeling the emotions of something versus it happening in the physical. It's pretty awesome! Not having an intention results in moving through life on autopilot. The unconscious mind controls autopilot. So, short version: clear the muck and old nonsense that is *not* you and never was in the first place.

What self-care, routines, and habits do you have to maintain good health?

I am a fitness junky and love all things health! I am all about six-day per-week workouts and for me, health and fitness is a lifestyle. I use a combination of fitness, energy work, healthy eating, loads of water (I drink a gallon of water a day), and meditation to stay grounded and in the highest vibe possible. I am no stranger to off days—we are human. It happens sometimes.

I work only in high-vibe energies (divine consciousness/source/universal consciousness/superconscious). The intention is to simply release *resistance* to what we want to create. There is no need to problem solve or do anything related to "fixing."

Learning to work with the energy of the superconscious is life-changing! The superconscious is the part of you (all of us) created and connected to all memory and can treat resistance in the form of beliefs, emotion, family history (genetic encodings passed down), parts/personalities, body systems, and so on. Working with the superconscious is simply about shifting pain into wisdom. I like to use the metaphor of a football field. Picture a football field with gopher holes and mounds of dirt (the painful experience or charge) throughout the field. The gopher holes symbolize resistance creating blocks in your life. With the help from superconscious, we simply brush the dirt back into the hole with a feather so you can play freely in the field with no mess or icky triggers holding you back.

I've learned we can have many parts working in conflict (i.e., one part wants a soul-mate relationship, and another part is hurt so deeply it does everything to protect from that pain again, ultimately sabotaging the relationship). We want to have all parts and personalities in one main unit. This mono-personality functions more efficiently and creates a flow for you to take inspired action toward your true choices easily. If we have one unit working together, this prevents oscillation and stuck choices so you take action without parts fighting against one another. All parts need to integrate as one. The superconscious is a field of energy we all have access to. Connecting with the superconscious and using energy work to rewire and release the things keeping me stuck has entirely changed my life. It's why I am here and why part of this book exists today. I am so passionate about this work and now use it in my business with my clients to help them rapidly uplevel.

What is the most worthwhile investment you have made for your business?

Investing in *myself* as it relates to my business! Period. The first coach I hired? Whew, *way* outside my financial comfort zone. I saw her on a Facebook video, and I was drawn to it. Something about her energy resonated with me, and I had this overwhelming feeling: *I am going to work with her.* (Those are the soul nudges and downloads we are meant to listen to, by the way.) I had a call with her, and she told me about her programs.

I was all in—until she told me the investment. My body cringed a little bit. No, it cringed a lot—sweaty palms, the whole bit. That part of me was still playing small—"Um, $11,000 for coaching? We can't afford that! What are you thinking, Amanda? That's insane." A part of me knew I was meant to work with her and had already decided to go all in. I got off the phone and ended it thinking, *I know I will work with her, and I will figure it out.* Her beautiful, non-pressure energy was super appealing and added to my *hell yes*. She was kind and said, "I'm here when you're ready. Set the intention for it to happen, and it will all unfold."

I had never experienced such ease in a "sales" call. This interaction taught me several things I never forgot. I thought, *This is how I will show up in my business!* She knew her worth and did not attempt to hard sell or pressure me into what I wasn't ready for at that moment.

High-pressure sales always felt so off. For example: You go on a date with a potential partner (date one, I might add). They tell you all the reasons you should pick them, and want a decision at that moment (gag). No, no, and no! Nurture the relationship. Let it evolve naturally. Let it resonate and be a *hell yes* for both parties. Feel the difference? For some reason with business, we sometimes get this wrong related to the outcomes we would like.

Only a month later, I signed up for her program and paid in full! I made the investment back within a couple of months. Now, spending that kind of money on a coach that I am a *hell yes* for is no longer uncomfortable. This goes back to our energetic set point (identity, identity, identity).

Wisdom Drop #6—We can make upleveling and investing in ourselves the norm, instead of energetically staying in the same space telling the same "I can't afford it" stories. Snail speed ahead (we do not have time for that, ladies). Be that next-level you, making next-level decisions.

That is the sweet spot for upleveling in business. I would make no such suggestion to spend your last penny or make a purchase that feels super unaligned. The investments in myself have *always* led to growth in my business and an energetic upleveling. My first investment led to the second one that was almost double the price of the first and initially outside my comfort zone. It felt right, so I did it anyway! You continue to uplevel your money container when you shift your mentality—would the future version of me make this high-vibe choice?

We often count ourselves out and unconsciously tell stories that the things we truly want and are meant for are out of our league. Bullshit. You align with your deepest desires and bring that amazing shit into your physical reality. Mindset shift, mindset shift, mindset shift. Identity, identity, identity. You've got this. I believe in you. Playing small is not serving anyone, and most importantly, it is not serving you.

If you lost everything today, what would you do for the next thirty days to generate income?

I would start setting intentions and results for what I want to create in my business. Reminder: intention and clarity are so powerful! When we claim and choose something, it plants the seeds in the universe. I know it may sound a bit far-fetched, but I can assure you it is a thing. I can say that because I have seen how transformative implementing this into my life has been. In a matter of months after learning this, I was able to quit my job (two of them), sell my home, and move to the place I have always wanted to be. I created it because I chose it and aligned my identity with already having it.

On a side note, if I lost everything, this would indicate to me there could be something in my identity structure that triggered this. I previously had serious money struggles. I had beliefs around money that repelled it as fast as it came in. It was rooted in my identity and beliefs that money was used as a way to manipulate; this goes far back to the way I perceived things growing up. I shifted this, and you can too (among other things)!

Wisdom Drop #7—The most important advice I can relay is: this life is supposed to be magnificent and lived to the fucking fullest. Living life to the fullest is unique to each one of us. Your business is a reflection of you. A reflection of your heart and soul.

I truly believe you intuitively know it's time to go all in on yourself and start living life on your terms. Pull back the curtains you hide behind and unapologetically unleash your heart and soul into this planet.

How can people connect with you?

I can be found at amandamonnier.com and on Instagram @amandamonnier.

THE JOURNEY OF BECOMING MORE PRESENT, LIVING A LIFE NONE OTHER THAN THE ONE YOU WERE BORN TO LIVE, IS THE KEY TO UNLOCKING PEAK PERFORMANCE.

Jill Phillips

CHAPTER 17

THE WINNING FORMULA BY JILL PHILLIPS

As a personal and professional development leader, I teach and coach entrepreneurs, professionals, leadership teams, and other coaches how to run their life and business with an endless source of clarity, confidence, and freedom.

Before 2013, I didn't know what this "coaching" thing was about. Honestly, it sounded a little fluffy. I have always specialized in supporting others to take steps toward their goals and dreams. But as for me, I was drowning with self-imposed expectations while juggling many hats and roles in my personal and professional world. People would comment on how I seemed to have it all together, which was flattering, but I felt like a total fraud inside. I continued to build up a life on the outside to mask the chaos below.

In my midthirties, I thought I had missed the boat. Most of my peers were invested in a full-time career, but my path started differently. A few months after graduating college, I had an unplanned pregnancy, leaving me with weighty and life-altering decisions. For better, for worse, I chose to marry and build a family over a career. I found intermittent part-time work while prioritizing a growing family and raising three children. Although rewarded with numerous upsides, motherhood didn't contribute to financial stability. Following a painful divorce, I went into survival mode, initially working four jobs just to get back on my feet.

I remarried a widower with two children of his own. We were a dynamic duo, supporting a blended family, one kid short of being the Brady Bunch. Blessed in numerous ways, there were stressful challenges we never could have anticipated. I blew any chance of receiving a mother of the year award with more "mom bombs" than gold stars by my name. Once again, I felt I was in over my head trying to survive.

I had support from family and friends, but no one could rescue me. Was this just life? Was this normal? Was the idea of finding happiness, freedom, and fulfillment an illusion, or was there more? I kept waiting for outside circumstances to change, thinking happiness and opportunity were just around the corner. I began to believe this was as good as it gets and found myself with even more guilt, pain, and despair.

"Wherever you go, there you will be" was a truth bomb that drew my curiosity. I knew something had to change, and it was me. I read dozens of self-help books, but this seemed to require a deeper level of serious soul-searching. But how? I loved Marianne Williamson's quote about how we are meant to shine, but was that in the cards for me? There had to be more to life, and if not, I would have to learn to be satisfied with the one I had. More afraid of the status quo than change, I hopped off the fence of indecision, took a leap of faith, and began working with a coach.

It didn't take long to realize there was nothing fluffy about it! I (my ego) was reluctant to receive support, but I found I don't always have to know *how*; finding a "who" to the "how" by being open created an abundance of possibilities. I discovered I was a professional martyr who had sacrificed my wants and needs for others for many years, causing me to lose sight of my personal and professional goals and dreams. I wasn't even sure I knew what they were anymore. It felt scary yet adventurous as I uncovered my truth, awakening desires and dormant dreams.

Coaching was everything I didn't know I needed and helped me gain clarity toward what I wanted. I began taking steps toward creating my new future instead of reacting to it. Confidence, clarity, and freedom showed up in unimaginable ways. I realized the power was within me all along, and it was time to take charge of my life, my relationships, my dreams, and my newfound exciting future. After all, it's never too late to live happily ever after."

One of my dreams was to do what I love, with people I enjoy spending time with, having a positive impact while creating a flexible schedule, and be compensated for it. I felt a nudge at a soul level that coaching was my future, so I started training right away. I was confident I could do it with entrepreneurial roots and a few network marketing escapades under my belt. My background in psychology—a degree in communication disorders and teaching—provided a powerful foundation that added enormous value to my coaching practice. Success, by no means, arrived on my doorstep overnight. My story comes with a collection of years of attending the school of hard knocks and dedication to lifelong learning.

Discovering my dream and taking action were two separate things. The taste of confidence was met with the "F" word: fear. It seemed incredibly selfish to abandon my number one role as a mother and wife to pursue my dream. I often felt judged by others and interpreted their fear as my own. Missing the boat, being too old, losing the respect of my children and friends, and even the fear of dissolving my second marriage were enough to stop me in my selfish pursuit of following a risky dream.

My greatest evolution was reconnecting with my greatest asset: my soul. As I gained insight and tools to navigate the mental chatter, I tapped into an infinite resource that I had a taste of in the past but didn't fully understand. I discovered ways to access this powerful gift that has since catapulted my success in starting a business, living some of my wildest dreams, allowing me to be an even better mother, and strengthening my marriage. I realized I didn't have to sacrifice one for the other with my new "and" mentality rather than my old "or" mentality.

Differentiating between selfishness and self-care was a pivotal point. Filling my cup and putting my oxygen mask on first was a nonnegotiable that allowed me to serve others from my overflow versus the survival-based state of depletion. Creating new interdependent boundaries and saying no was scary for the people-pleaser part of me. But now, I had new tools to navigate my emotions and mind to help make proactive decisions. Saying yes to myself was where things began to take off. Maybe I hadn't missed the boat after all.

Professional training offered transformational tools, but it was up to me to do the rest. Over time, I had a revolving clientele and discovered a niche working with entrepreneurs, superachievers, professionals, and other high performers who were in the midst of a tremendous growth spurt, trying to break through the next ceiling of success. I discovered an uncanny similarity between the obstacles in life and business. What shows up in one area will show up in every area, for better or worse. I grew my business by referrals and results, but I made a startling discovery three years into coaching. I wasn't running a business. I was offering a service. I had an incredible foundation, but now I was faced with a new challenge. It was time to take the heart and soul (my service) to another level with a system and strategy. Yet again, I was called to grow.

Over time, my clients began inviting me to work with their multimillion-dollar organizations, but I lacked the confidence and clarity of knowing where to start. I decided to embrace a new challenge and found a holistic business operating system program that ignited something in my soul. I hopped on a plane, went through intensive training, and have been serving clients with life and business coaching since. That may sound simple, but it was not easy. Looking back, I would do it all over again, heeding the rabbit holes that threatened to put a lid on my happiness and success.

What is your *why* or purpose for your business?

My beautiful children were the reason I began this journey. My *why* has evolved to helping others become more connected and inspired, bringing deeper meaning to the world around us for positive ripples of change. Helping people rebuild their identity from who they are versus what they do unlocks human potential, bringing abundance and prosperity to every area in life and business. The journey of becoming more present, living a life none other than the one you were born to live, is the key to unlocking peak performance. With this foundation, all things are possible.

The greatest tragedy is for someone to die with the music still inside them, not realizing or bringing their gifts and talents to the world. You won't miss the boat when you take time to invest in yourself and gain knowledge and tools that will help you not just survive but thrive in whatever comes at you in life or business.

What are the biggest mistakes you see new entrepreneurs making?

Being an entrepreneur is tough, but extremely rewarding. There's debate as to whether entrepreneurs are made or born. What is not arguable is that there's not a lot of training on how to live an entrepreneurial life and make costly decisions. What gives entrepreneurs their drive to succeed is, in turn, an invitation for the soul's evolution. The only boat to be missed is not taking the opportunity to learn, grow, and evolve.

Before looking at entrepreneurial mistakes, note that there are two pillars of success that will transform your life and business from the inside out when practiced. There are no magic pills, no fluff or rah-rah here. Instead, you will find timeless principles that will help you on your journey. But the first big decision you must make is saying yes to investing in yourself.

Truth bomb: You cannot help anyone else unless you help yourself. To help yourself, you must know yourself, which is the evolving journey of self-mastery. Personal development is professional development, and your level of success will rarely surpass your level of personal development. Self-mastery isn't about achieving perfection or being a guru, but being a committed practitioner of the psychic push-ups that will repay you in countless ways in your life and your business.

Pillar #1: Self-belief

Self-belief is a positive feeling of the deep existence within you that knows you are capable of anything. You are unstoppable. You feel empowered, confident, and fueled with good vibes in the face of challenges and problems. Self-belief comes by aligning your thoughts, words, and actions, which leads to internal stability, also known as congruence.

While self-belief is important for all, entrepreneurs know that it takes enormous guts and self-belief to bare your vision and soul to the world. You will encounter perceived failures, rejections, and judgment that leave you doubting yourself and your decisions. This is what makes this the first pillar of success.

Pillar #2: Self-compassion

Self-compassion is more effective than self-criticism because its driving force is love, not fear. Unlike self-criticism, which asks if you are enough, self-compassion finds where you are enough and helps you lead with greater confidence, clarity, and empathy.

This is tricky, especially for entrepreneurs, because self-reflection is imperative for growth. Entrepreneurs are constantly evaluating, predicting, and pivoting. Without a strategy, it opens Pandora's box for the inner critic and perfectionist to hijack your confidence and leave you with self-doubt and confusion.

Self-compassion is a practiced skill of witnessing versus judging your actions or performance. Be sure to add a healthy dose of self-acknowledgment and gratitude along the way. Entrepreneurs often get lost in the destination without understanding the transformative power of gratitude and being in the now. Appreciating where you are and being eager for what's next while speaking an affirmative language is the secret sauce that channels your focus toward what you want more than what you don't.

Where your attention goes, energy flows, and what you focus on grows! So be careful with your words and how you respond to yourself, because your mind, body, and soul are listening and responding to what you believe. What you acknowledge gets repeated, so be sure to lean on this pillar with self and others as part of a winning formula for success.

Here's what you *won't* get in Entrepreneurialism Leadership 101, but need to understand:

1. Know Fear

Entrepreneurs are thought to be fearless—well, that's a lie. Successful people are not absent from fear. It's how they handle it that matters, which is why it's imperative to understand it. Entrepreneurs are human, and our human brain was designed around keeping us safe. With the weight on entrepreneurs' shoulders, fears are larger and even more real.

Here's a hardcore truth: your business grows as much as you do. You will need a strategy to manage your fear. Learning basic neuroscience offers insight into accessing the brain's CEO part (pre-neocortex) that guides powerful decision-making. On the contrary, when fear strikes, the reptilian part of the brain goes into survival mode, igniting a fight, flight, or freeze response. This mode triggers undesirable thoughts, feelings, and emotions that produce self-limiting beliefs. In other words, when people are under stress, they do weird stuff and act with uncharacteristic-like behaviors that are counterproductive and often destructive.

Without learning how to manage your emotions and how to utilize your brain to work for you, you will not be in business for very long or at least in a fulfilling or successful one. By learning to utilize the brain, you can open space for your soul to make decisions and create soul-utions.

There's a lot to be learned through science, transformational psychology, and ancient wisdom. Reading books, attending seminars, and listening to podcasts are good tools for self-development, but it just becomes a piece of information if we cannot apply it. For courageous growth seekers wanting to take greater control of their life and outcomes: working with a professional coach can help you learn new strategies to manage your IQ, EQ, and SQ (soul intelligence) while uncovering subconscious patterns and blind spots that keep you on the hamster wheel, evading success. Coaching will propel you forward farther and faster than you could on your own.

2. Imposter Syndrome

Many entrepreneurs suffer in isolation, experiencing sadness, anxiety, and anger, which compromises performance. The pesky mind chatter of ego says you should figure it all out and that your quality problems are not as important as the deeper issues needed to be solved in the world. Your sanity is at stake, leaving you to question if you need psychotherapy. It feels as if there's nowhere to go and no way out, but you're determined not to quit. After all, you are a creative entrepreneur, and everything is "figureoutable."

Left unmanaged, the mind chatter gets louder and carries you into the rabbit hole. "Who do you think you are to have this kind of success? You can't do that. You're not an expert. You're too young. You're too old. You'll lose your family and friends if you work at that pace. If you fail, people will be waiting in line to say, 'I told you so.'" Believing the chatter causes you to focus on your mistakes instead of possibilities, most often on a subconscious level. Worse yet, it will keep you believing you don't deserve to have success or fun.

The voices are the gateway for the emotional roller coaster of imposter syndrome. Imposter syndrome is real and can ring truest amid tough and lonely times. The inner critic and perfectionist can take you out if you do not have insight into your brain and tools to manage your mind, emotions, and business.

Most commonly, people avoid, suppress, distract, or compartmentalize the voices and pain. Putting duct tape and twine around your problems and feelings leads to a temporary solution or quick fix but will continue to bubble up until you take care of the issue at the root cause.

A soul strategy offers a way to manage stress and setbacks by seeing it for what it is, which is temporary and not the end of the world. A self-mastery practitioner will recognize the mind's tricks, knowing it's not you who is a failure. It's just a part of self that feels this way. This powerful distinction offers a way to have a healthy, open dialogue with the part that feels this way (which is not you). With the countless hats and roles of an entrepreneur, it's imperative to root yourself in who you truly are at a core level to un-blend from these parts. This practice will dissipate the ego that keeps you stuck and frustrated.

3. Work-Life Balance?

The majority of my speaking requests are on the topic of work-life balance. Balance is especially challenging for owners and entrepreneurs. While pushing hard to make your business a success, it's easy to lose sight of other important things like family and health.

Here's the bottom line: Spending equal amounts of time in work and life is not realistic or attainable, which are two parts of a SMART goal. On a logical level, people know this, but it doesn't stop the fairy tale of striving for this unattainable dream. This is one of the greatest myths that keep people, especially entrepreneurs, from finding happiness. Determined to debunk this unrealistic goal, I collected information from my entrepreneurial clients, listening at a deeper level to find what their soul was calling for.

What I found was this: Most people spend more time at work than at home, especially entrepreneurs. The desire to be seen, heard, and valued is strong. Knowing this is valuable when you have employees, but as for an entrepreneur, you're often on your own, having to find affirmation from within.

Ultimately, entrepreneurs are problem solvers who channel their creative energy to make decisions with clarity and focus. They desire to be productive doing what they are best at; they are able to unplug their mind, be present, and enjoy spending time with people they love with time to pursue other interests and passions. Sadly, divorce rates of entrepreneurs are high, as they often do not have the support or training that personal development offers, leaving home life and relationships in trouble. Their business suffers for it. While work-life balance in itself is a myth, the feeling is attainable!

4. Who Am I?

Remember you are a human BEing, not a human DOing. Most people operate with a backward strategy: "If I do XYZ, then I will have XYZ, and then I will be happy, or rich, or successful." This creates a profound barrier to growth and will keep you on the hamster wheel of despair.

Leading with your BEing versus DOing will increase your success rate with liberating upsides. I've helped numerous people unlock confidence, clarity, and freedom utilizing the DO-BE-HAVE model. Practicing the BE-DO-HAVE model versus the DO-HAVE-BE method is a powerful strategy that can unlock greater clarity, confidence, and freedom. It can release the invisible walls holding people back from true abundance and having more in life and business.

5. Have a Strategy

Hitting the ceiling is a way nature calls us to grow. To grow, we must evolve. When we grow and evolve, the ego (fear) fights hard. Remember that on the other side of a breakdown is a breakthrough. So when the going gets tough, the tough go back to the basics. Here are a few ways to go back to the basics for a breakthrough:

- Simplify. Keep it simple (a challenge for the entrepreneurial brain).
- Focus on the next step, not *all* of the steps.

- Prioritize and learn to say no.
- Delegate the stuff you don't like and don't excel at.
- Do a checkup to see if your intention, values, and needs are in alignment.
- Take clarity breaks often.

WARNING: "Vision without action is hallucination," Thomas Edison said. Entrepreneurs, new or experienced, lose focus with new ideas also known as the "shiny stuff." Most entrepreneurs are visionary, which means they're great with the big picture and never have a shortage of ideas. The biggest challenge is taking the vision to the ground and executing it. The struggle in the details and execution can lead to procrastination and distraction known as performance paralyzation.

To combat this phenomenon, save you valuable time, and hold on to some level of sanity, here are a few nonnegotiables to add to your strategy, allowing this to be a filter that guides your decision-making. While it sounds simple, go deep. Without this guide, you will financially, mentally, and emotionally deplete yourself and never achieve your vision:

- Define your core values (your soul values).
- Know your focus.
- Have a sales/marketing plan.
- Know your three-year picture, one-year goals, and quarterly goals.
- Create an ongoing issue list to free your mind for higher-order thinking.
- Have accountability.

6. Just Breathe

Almost everything will work again if you unplug it for a few minutes, including you. Entrepreneurial ideas are often delivered in a state of nonresistance, also called *receiving*. The law of reciprocity, known as the flow in life, is about giving and receiving. One way to receive is to be still and know. Just breathe.

Taking a break may sound counterproductive, but it's a nonnegotiable for success. A break can be a few intentional deep breaths, a nature walk, journaling, or a vacation, just to name a few. Taking a breath or a break allows you to stop DOing, and just BE.

The most underestimated break is the power of a few deep breaths. The breath cycle is on autopilot. Intentionally pausing to take conscious breaths is one of the most effective ways to lower everyday stress. Practicing conscious breath deactivates the autonomic nervous fight-or-flight system and induces the parasynthetic response, turning up calmness and mental clarity. Breathing is one of our five common senses we can utilize to get back to the basics at a soul level. Unfortunately, using common sense is said not to be all that common, especially in the world of distractions we live in.

When you create a habit of taking clarity breaks every day, even just for five minutes, your days start looking different. Your cortisol (stress) levels lower, which also has the benefit of helping to lose a few extra pounds. Life is made up of how you spend your days. How you spend your days becomes how you live your life. This practice is a game changer for the mind, body, soul, and your business!

7. Find Satisfaction

The song "(I Can't Get No) Satisfaction" is a common sentiment of an entrepreneur. As you strive for success, stop and ask yourself, often: When is "good enough" *good enough* and how much is enough? Contradictory to the hunger and drive of an entrepreneur, the "good enough" question may sound ridiculous. There is nothing wrong with striving for more, but if you don't know what your sweet spot is by defining your vision of success, you may never get that satisfaction.

A key distinction often missed is that it's not just about the six-figure business. It's who you become while creating this business. Your business is a playing field for your soul print and expansion.

So be sure to bring your soul, intuition, and intention to align with your system and strategy to unlock your inevitable success.

If you lost everything today, what would you do for the next thirty days to generate income?

I'd go back to the basics, because when the going gets tough, the tough go back to the basics. I'd start with a clarity break so I can be open to receiving soul-utions.

With coaching as the number one skill set of the twenty-first century, there are countless ways to expand, including mastermind groups, executive coaching, training coaches, personal and professional curriculum development, retreats, speaking engagements, and more!

How can people connect with you?

I can be reached by email at jill@jillphillipscoaching.com.

SUCCESS IS DOING WHAT I WANT, WHERE I WANT, WHEN I WANT, AND WITH WHOM I WANT.

Cristina Rodriguez

CHAPTER 18

NICHING UP TO SEVEN FIGURES BY CRISTINA RODRIGUEZ

On March 15, 1993, I found out why I was put here on earth. It was a Monday (probably one of the many reasons why I love Mondays so much—don't all entrepreneurs?), and I was eight years old. I had recently moved from the "dirty Jerz" to Tampa, Florida, and was trying to find my place in a brand-new city, at a brand-new school, with brand-new kids.

I wasn't like the others. I was a tomboy who preferred Nikes over heels and baseball hats over flat ironing my hair. I had a smart mouth and was an only child (with only-child syndrome). As an only child, you tend to live in your own little world and you learn quickly to be happy in your own company, with your thoughts, and with your stuffed animals. I truly believe that being an only child has helped me through the darkest times of my entrepreneurial journey. On those days and nights when you are all alone, just you and your ideas (and only you to follow through on them), you've got to be comfortable in your skin; otherwise, imposter syndrome has a tendency to start creeping in and taking over.

As a kid, I had tried finding my place in the world with gymnastics and baseball. Still, it wasn't until I stepped into the martial arts dojo on that life-changing day in 1993 that I found my true purpose in life and what would eventually become the niche that I would build a seven-figure empire off of.

I call moments like the one I had in March 1993 "moments of impact." It's these moments of impact that define our story and help us write and color in the chapters. We all have them. They are the defining moments in our lives that become Polaroids in our minds. They become the building blocks of our companies, relationships, and the stories that we will tell our grandchildren.

In this chapter, I would like to share the moments of impact that I have had in my journey of becoming a seven-figure entrepreneur in hopes that it will inspire you, teach you, and prove to you the power of homing in on and owning your niche.

Niche—what a funny-sounding word pronounced in one of two ways. If you look it up in the dictionary, as a noun, it states, "A comfortable or suitable position in life or employment" and also "A specialized segment of the market for a particular kind of product or service."

It can be used synonymously with your calling, vocation, or métier (a French borrowing acquired by English speakers in the late eighteenth century; typically implies a calling for which one feels especially fitted).

I'm sure you've been told that you should "find a niche if you want to succeed in business as an entrepreneur." And while I believe you can succeed without specializing in a specific niche, it's so much easier when you "niche down." Martial arts is the niche market that I chose to build a seven-figure empire on. Have you chosen yours?

I believe that training in martial arts is ultimately a vehicle to reaching one's human potential, and it has been the main part of my life for nearly three decades. It has provided me with comfort, safety, fitness, and friends and now provides my family with an income that we always dreamed possible.

Most people open up martial arts schools because they have a passion for teaching martial arts and want to share that with others.

Unfortunately, most martial arts school owners are dead broke. I'm all about turning your passion into your income—but that income better not have a ceiling.

I started "working" at my Tae Kwon Do school when I was ten years old by helping to assist classes. At age eleven, I earned my black belt; at fifteen, I was officially hired as an assistant instructor; and by age eighteen, I was the first female head instructor in the school's thirty-year history.

Talk about breaking glass ceilings as opposed to fitting in glass slippers.

I knew from that very first day when I stepped into the martial arts school that I would own my academy one day. I remember sitting in my room in my preteen years, all alone, drawing blueprints of what my dream school would look like. I spent my weeks at the academy for four hours a day. I spent my weekends teaching martial arts classes in my room to my stuffed animals. Every single talent show from grade school to high school, I performed martial arts. I knew in my soul and in my heart that I would be able to change people's lives with my venture, and I ignored the haters (including family members).

I went to the University of South Florida to obtain my degree in elementary education with the goal of opening my own martial arts school and to use my degree to help me impact more kids in the Tampa Bay community. During my time at USF, I started training at a Brazilian jiu jitsu school and eventually worked full-time there as the kids' head instructor and manager.

Literally every job I have ever had has been in a martial arts school. I've been a janitor, assistant instructor, head instructor, manager, and owner (with the exception of one summer when I worked at Chuck E. Cheese and was paid $5.50 per hour to dress up as the rat. It was that summer when I was convinced being an entrepreneur was the way to go).

While I was going to USF, I was also getting my entrepreneurial education at the jiu jitsu school that I was teaching at and managing.

Having the opportunity to manage the academy taught me so many great lessons on what to do (and more importantly what not to do) when it was time to open up my school. I worked for very little money, but most people who become rich ultimately work to learn and not for the money.

My childhood dream of opening my own martial arts academy came to fruition on September 22, 2012. It was the day I also earned my Brazilian Jiu-Jitsu black belt. If you know anything about martial arts, then you know that jiu jitsu is one of the hardest styles. On average, it takes about ten years to get a black belt. It's similar to wrestling in that it teaches you how to defend yourself on the ground (something that I truly believe all women should learn how to do—but that's a story for another book). I was the first and remain the only female to have earned a Brazilian jiu jitsu black belt under my instructor who has been teaching for over twenty years.

Owning and operating a brick-and-mortar martial arts business with my wife, Stephanie, for almost a decade has provided some of the greatest business lessons I ever could have asked for.

As our martial arts school continued to grow, hiring rock-star team members became an integral part of our business. As much as I love martial arts, I don't want to be at my academy all day. Been there, done that, got burnt out.

In three short years, we were able to grow our martial arts academy to a half-million-dollar company, and it caught the eye of many other martial arts school owners. They started asking how we became so successful, so quickly (especially having two women at the helm in a male-dominated industry).

This is where the start of my internet marketing career took off and where focusing on my specific niche helped me to build a seven-figure empire. I had studied internet marketing while I was operating my instructor's school to help him build *his* school, knowing my newfound knowledge would help me build *my* school one day. I specifically fell in love with running Facebook ads. The fact that I could open my laptop, launch a campaign, and within an hour have viable leads excited me (and my bank account).

I immersed myself in learning everything I could about internet marketing: building funnels, landing pages, and sales pages; learning copywriting; creating follow-up email/SMS automation; placing ads; reading metrics; and the list goes on and on. I dedicated myself to becoming a skill collector (and I still do to this day). And those skills, although time-consuming and hard to learn, ultimately paid off by helping me launch several online businesses.

The very first course I ever launched was called the Perfect Kids Jiu-Jitsu Class Course. I created it and launched it on Black Friday in 2016. I can remember it clear as day. I was down in Del Ray, Florida, visiting my biological dad, and we were set to launch at 5:00 A.M. on Black Friday. I remember waking up to the sound of a Stripe notification telling me that we made our first sale.

The entire morning, day, and into the night, my phone just kept going off, notifying me of sale after sale after sale. It was the most amazing and addicting feeling I've ever had. You see, owning a brick-and-mortar service-based business meant that for us to make money, someone had to be in the business servicing people. With an online business, it's completely different. You can literally make money while you sleep.

The success of my first online course launch led me to build out an entire online platform in ClickFunnels (which I then moved to Kajabi and later moved to Teachable) called the Kids Jitz Academy. It was an online training and curriculum platform for martial arts school owners who wanted to improve their kids' programs. The best part? It was a recurring payment model, and it was the first of its kind in our industry.

It was incredibly successful with hundreds of school owners joining, and the launch of the Kids Jitz Academy then led me to launch my group coaching mastermind for school owners called the A-Team Mastermind. Working one-on-one and in a group coaching setting allowed me to make a greater impact in our industry.

Have you ever thought about what the number one question is that people ask their business coaches? It's usually surrounding the topic of, "How can I get more clients?" Doesn't matter what the niche is; we know to have a successful business, you've got to have clients.

This constant question that I was getting always led me to teach them how I was able to grow my school so quickly, which was through online marketing. As I worked with more and more school owners, I saw this trend over and over again. So I started teaching them how to use digital marketing to grow their schools. I launched an eight-week marketing mastermind course that taught school owners how to launch their Facebook ads, how to use Instagram to grow their local following, and how to launch Google Ads.

The problem I ran into . . . it's freaking *tough* for the average school owner! In an ever-changing digital world, technology is always evolving, platforms are always updating, and if you're not computer savvy, it's enough to make you want to rip your hair out. I moved from the "done with you" model to the "done for you" model when I launched my digital marketing agency (Grow Pro Agency) in March 2019. Oftentimes, it's better to ask "Who can do this for me?" not "How can I do this?"

At my agency, we are currently running Facebook, Instagram, Google, and YouTube ads for over 150 martial arts schools all over the world and just hit our seven-figure run rate, which took two years. We also offer social media management and database reactivation as part of our packages. I have a team of twelve rock stars, and we saw a 200 percent increase in total revenue from 2019 to 2020. That's right. We actually *grew* during the pandemic!

As my name started to get bigger and bigger in our industry, I was approached by the Martial Arts Industry Association (MAIA) and offered a position to be their digital marketing consultant. MAIA is the largest and oldest consulting company in the martial arts industry, and positioning myself with them has been one of the best B2B decisions I have ever made. It's a feeder program into my marketing agency and has positioned me as an expert in our industry. I write articles for the top martial arts magazine every quarterly edition. They have put me on the cover and just invited me to be the cohost for the 2021 Martial Arts SuperShow (the biggest conference in our industry).

Our martial arts school, Gracie PAC, is thriving after the pandemic nearly cost us one-third of our members. We are currently located in a five-thousand-square-foot facility in Tampa and have averaged around three hundred members. My wife and I spend about two hours a week maintaining it due to us having a rock-star team in place.

Some leaders say that if you don't know how to manage $10,000, then you're not going to know how to manage $10,000,000. With the success of our companies, it was imperative that we made wise decisions regarding our future and our retirement. My wife and I decided to focus on real estate to help us grow our wealth, and in 2020, we started our first real estate holding company, NestRock LLC, and purchased our first commercial building.

Purchasing the building was a great choice for us, as we were renting out office space for our marketing agency. So now we had somewhere we could put our growing team of twelve employees. The cherry on top: we have a tenant in the second suite whose rent covers our mortgage.

Success is doing what I want, where I want, when I want, and with whom I want. And that's why I became an entrepreneur. I believe that life is better with choices. And living an entrepreneurial lifestyle means you have a lot more potential choices and freedom. In the following questions, I will take my knowledge of owning four businesses to help you fast-track your success.

Let's dive in.

What is your *why* or purpose for your business?

Most people will probably answer this question with their company mission statement, but I will answer it a little bit differently.

As the CEO of my companies, if my mojo is off, everything is going to be off. It's said that the "fish stinks from the head," so I protect my energy, my mojo, my *why* (or whatever else you want to call it) at all costs. My *why* is something that I write down every single day in my journal. It's constantly in front of me and at the top of my mind so that on the days when I might not feel like doing something, this puts that little inner bitch to rest.

My reason *why* is to have financial freedom so I can work when I want to and where I want to, so I can spend more time with my family, so we can travel the world, so we can share life's best experiences together, so I have no regrets on my deathbed, so I will have lived my best life with the people I love. If you are truly curious about the *why* or mission statement of my companies, here they are:

- Gracie PAC MMA: We inspire others to discover their hidden potential.
- Grow Pro Agency: We help business owners gain the freedom to do what they love.
- The A-Team Mastermind: We help turn your passion into an income-generating machine.
- NestRock LLC: We positively impact our family tree.

What are the biggest mistakes you see new entrepreneurs making?

I recently aired an episode of my podcast (*Elevate: Empowering Entrepreneurs*) on this exact topic after listening to one of my mentors teach on this. There are three huge mistakes that entrepreneurs make, including me. So let's break these three mistakes down.

Mistake #1—Entrepreneurs do not hire fast enough.

I will dive into this in one of the future questions because this has been my Achilles' heel for nearly the past decade. Most people believe that "once I make enough money, I will hire someone to help me." The truth is, you hire someone to help you so you *can* make the extra money.

Often, we look at hiring someone and how it will affect us in the immediate month or months. When in actuality, we should look at it in an annual sense or a long-term play. For example, if you hire someone to help you for $15 per hour for twenty hours per week, this will cost you $1,200 per month. More than likely, if you're just getting started, you will probably take some of this out of your personal profits for the first month or two.

But if we look at this as a long-term play, and if you train this person properly, within a month or two, they should be able to either strum up business for you to cover their costs or they will be able to take some items off your plate so you can focus on tasks that have a direct impact to the bottom line (more on this later). I believe that as an entrepreneur, if you want to be able to be successful, you've got to be able to manage three things:

1. Cash flow,
2. Thoughts, and
3. Personalities.

While growing an empire might not be one of your personal goals, it is one of mine, and because of this, I have had to become a master at managing personalities with having twenty total employees at the time of this writing. No matter where you are in your business, hiring, firing, and managing personalities is always going to be something you will have to work on.

Every single time that I have made a smart hire, my companies have grown. We can't do it all—no matter how much of a superwoman you are. You've got to hire help, align your employees with your vision, and train them to become better human beings. I get asked often, "Aren't you worried that you're going to spend all this time and energy and money investing in people who are one day going to leave?"

My response is: "What is the other choice? Don't train them and hope they stay?"

My companies are here to do more than just help our clients; they're here to help level up our team and their lives. It's my job to take care of my team members—it's their job to take care of our clients. The longer you wait to hire someone to help you, the longer you are putting off accomplishing your goals.

Mistake #2—Entrepreneurs do not reinvest their profits into marketing.

One of my favorite quotes from Henry Ford is, "A man who stops advertising to save money is like a man who stops a clock to save time." Marketing and advertising are an integral part of any successful business, and not having "enough money" to market or advertise is just not a viable excuse. In our business, we always have two choices to make:

1. Learn how to do it yourself and spend your time and energy.
2. Hire someone else to do it and spend your money.

If you don't have the money to advertise and market, you need to put in your time and energy and work on organic strategies to gain more business to reinvest the profits back into the marketing. Peter Drucker eloquently said, "All you need is innovation and marketing." If you don't have the money to market, then you better get innovative!

Mistake #3—Entrepreneurs do not hire a mentor fast enough.

I believe there are two ways to fast-track your success:

1. Hire a mentor.
2. Get an accountability partner.

In every single area of my life that I want to improve on, I have a mentor. I have a mentor for keeping my marriage strong. I have a mentor for being the best parent that I can be. I have a mentor for my martial arts business. I have a mentor for my agency. I have a mentor for my consulting business. I have a mentor for keeping my fitness and health on track. I have a mentor for investing.

Often, we say, "I will hire a mentor when I have enough money." The right mentor can help you make "enough money" in one session together. So how do you find the right mentor? You opt in, go through their funnel, get on a discovery call, and see if your core values are in line.

There are so many successful people out there in all the different areas of your life. And there are many different ways to become successful in our businesses. For me, the most important is that they have a proven track record of getting to where I want to go and that our core values are in line. If those two boxes are checked, I hire them.

Which activities do you perform that generate the majority of your revenue?

As my businesses have grown and evolved, the activities I have focused on generating the majority of my revenue have changed over the years. I've gone from "working in the business" to "working on the business." (If you haven't read *The E-Myth* by Michael Gerber, it's in my top five business books for entrepreneurs.)

As I create my "rocks" (quarterly projects) each quarter and break them down into monthly and weekly goals, the question I always ask myself is: *Does this have a direct effect on the bottom line?* If the answer is no, then it's something that needs to be delegated. If the answer is yes, then it's okay for me to move forward on those tasks to complete the project.

Sales are the lifeblood of any business. No sales equals no business. Simple, yes. Easy, not always. Oftentimes, and I am going to generalize here for a minute, we women have a tendency to focus on the little itty-bitty details of our businesses instead of focusing on the most important aspect: getting more sales. So many people have such a derogatory feeling about the word *sales*. If that's you, just think of it as service because making a sale is ultimately that: providing a service to someone.

I spend the majority of my time finding ways for our company to grow, and to grow, we've got to make more sales. My focus is on developing better relationships and aligning with other people and businesses in our industry (networking), teaching my team to become better at sales and fulfillment (training), and tracking our KPIs (finance) so I can make data-driven decisions in my companies.

If you ever walked into one of my businesses, within a short period, you would hear me declare: "Math is the path."

Despite being a straight A student, I always struggled in math classes and it did not come easy for me. I learned early on (through my mentors) the importance of tracking your stats and making data-driven (not emotional) decisions. Your business's numbers are actually giving you a road map to where you need to focus your efforts. Pay attention to the numbers.

What is your biggest day-to-day struggle in running your business?

I come from what some would call a privileged family at first glance—but when you dig deeper, I come from a family of immigrants and hard workers. My grandparents on both sides immigrated to New York from Puerto Rico with nothing in their pockets. They worked two to three jobs each to provide my parents with a life better than theirs. A strong, hard work ethic is in my blood and is what I consider one of my superpowers.

It's a funny thing, superpowers. Often, they can end up becoming your Achilles' heel if you're not careful. Hard work is great, but it can only get you so far since there are only twenty-four hours in a day.

A hard work ethic is the biggest struggle that I deal with on a day-to-day basis with running my companies. The work will never end. There will always be more ideas, and often businesses fail not due to a lack of ideas, but due to trying to implement too many!

My biggest day-to-day struggle has always been my capabilities and willingness to do the work myself, especially if it's work that I enjoy. I constantly have to remind myself that just because I have the skill set to do something and the willingness to do it doesn't mean that that's where I should be focusing my efforts.

What have you found helps with blending your personal and professional life?

I will go against the grain here and say that I do not believe in work-life balance. Over the past decade of being an entrepreneur, I've taken courses, read books, and have tried just about everything to find "that balance."

I look at my work and my home life as more of a pendulum swinging from side to side than a balanced scale. When I'm at work, I'm 100 percent at work. When I'm at home, I'm 100 percent at home. That pendulum swings back and forth each day and allows me to be where my feet are.

I find that people who are searching for that balance between work and life end up in what Eben Pagan calls the "grey zone." That grey zone often finds its way into entrepreneurs' lives and can become one of the biggest hurdles to overcome.

So what is the grey zone? It's the times when you are at work and you think that you should be with your family, and it's the times when you are with your family and you are thinking about work.

Set up your day and your environment to completely focus on the tasks at hand when you are working and when you are resting.

What is the most worthwhile investment you have made for your business?

There are two:

1. The decision to marry my wife Stephanie was the most worthwhile investment that I made in my life and my business. If you and your spouse are not on the same page in regard to your business, you are going to be fighting a constant uphill battle. I was able to attract the perfect human being into my life who has provided me with the support we need to be able to make our dreams come true. Best investment if you ask me.
2. I spend over $3,000 every single month investing in my mentors. 'Nuff said.

If you lost everything today, what would you do for the next thirty days to generate income?

The reason why I am a self-proclaimed skill collector is that once you develop a skill, it's something that no one can take away from you. I believe that the rate of growth in our business is directly correlated with the number of skills we collect.

If I were to lose everything today, I would launch a course that would solve a problem that my list was having. I would use my business line of credit to purchase the necessary tools I would need to produce the course and would then leverage Facebook ads to sell the course.

Sometimes the best ideas are the simplest ideas.

How can people connect with you?

I can be found at facebook.com/CristinaLeeRodriguez.

DO ME A FAVOR: DO NOT LET IMPOSTER SYNDROME HOLD YOU BACK FOR ONE MINUTE LONGER. THERE ARE PEOPLE IN THIS WORLD WHO NEED YOU. CONSIDER IT A DISSERVICE NOT TO INVITE THOSE PEOPLE INTO YOUR WORLD.

Patty Rogers

CHAPTER 19

HIDDEN STRENGTH WITHIN BY PATTY ROGERS

Ever since I was a young girl, I've seen myself as a business owner. The type of business varied at different stages of my life. In my early twenties, it was a pedicure shop. My biweekly pedicure with a friend was a treat, and I enjoyed it thoroughly and considered the effort to start a shop of my own. Later in life, after planning my wedding, I went down the beginning stages of becoming a wedding planner. Weddings were happy events, so why wouldn't I want to be part of that happy event? Fast-forward a couple of years later, I became a mother. My daughter had long red hair, and drying the hair of a two-year-old with twin infants in the bath made me think of a better way. So, I created a product to help moms with bath time in a child-size towel for the head. It was called Girlie Locks. I had a patent pending and everything. These were all ideas that got various levels of my attention. Naturally, some got further along in the process than others.

I am the owner of B2B Digital Assistance. I've run this company for the last four years as the CEO and a mama boss. When people ask me what I do, I say, "I own a marketing and sales agency focusing on business automation." This is officially my third business, not counting all the ideas I previously shared with you.

It's been a journey and not necessarily always a pretty one.

We'll start with the story of the first business. My husband, our nine-month-old daughter, and I moved closer to family. We were in a new town, and it was time to start looking for daycare for our daughter. That's where I ran into my first challenge. I had worked hard to get our daughter on a great schedule, including two consistent naps.

It might not seem like a big deal, but it was important to me in those moments as a new mom. We ran into the same challenge with every provider we interviewed. When I mentioned her sleep schedule, I heard a similar response: "We'll just put her in the car while we go pick up the other kids from school, and she can nap while we're driving." My imagination went to some stranger driving an SUV full of kids ranging in age from newborn to school-age. My internal voice told me what to do: "Thanks, but no thanks."

As a family, we decided I would stay home with her. It was a logical choice, as we lived in California and daycare was expensive anyway and we could find time to bond. A good solution, right? Wrong! Let me say this next piece with the utmost respect and appreciation I possibly can: I like kids, and I'm a great mom, yet deep down, I knew I was not cut out to be a full-time stay-at-home mom. Again, I have tremendous respect for those who do it and make it look easy. Here's what happened during my short stint of being a stay-at-home mom: I questioned my own worth. I wasn't fulfilled, as I didn't feel like I contributed to my family in the ways I wanted to as a person. Working was always part of my identity. My mom worked full-time as a single mother. She seemed to effortlessly raise both my sister and me completely on her own. She made it look so easy. Never did I imagine not wanting to be a stay-at-home mom. It wasn't about worth; it was about fulfillment. As a strong woman, as a wife, and as a mother, I needed more to show up as my best self. At the time, I could not know it, but now I look back and see how naturally it feels to me to run my own company.

Business number one was born. You recall the problem. I couldn't find the type of daycare I was looking for. Pair that with my desire to find the best of both worlds. A flexible job that I operated provided the mental fulfillment I yearned for while staying home with my children. The math of the operation made total sense, so it was a go.

What was born was an in-home daycare. Mrs. Roger's neighborhood! Seriously, that was the company name, and I can hardly believe it as I type it now. What I noticed then was that I excelled with all the back-office stuff. The blueprint for success in the processes, the marketing, and overseeing daily operations. These carry over to what I love doing today. Back then, I even hired someone to run the front end of the business in taking care of other people's kids in my own house. Doing the daycare was *not* my favorite part of owning a daycare. By no means was I looking for a way out of childcare. When the universe's idea is different than yours, you get pregnant with twins, or at least I did. My daycare license was 50 percent occupied by my own three children and not a financially sustainable business model. Timing is so much in life. Around the same time, a colleague of my husband needed remote office work for his company. He wanted a virtual assistant and hired me to run the basic day-to-day operations. Daycare went away, and business number two was born!

That was the day of 1099 Assistant, or my virtual assistant company. I ran 1099 Assistant for nearly a decade. This first client introduced me to Infusionsoft, now called Keap. Around the eight-year mark, it was time for a pivot. This client was making changes in his own life. This was a clear opportunity. Originally, I'd operate my virtual assistant company and my Keap–certified partner company in parallel. With two companies, I had two suitors and I quickly realized I was creating complexity when I needed to simplify. What was needed was to delete or edit my services. With a simple list, I quickly identified areas that were clearly what I did best coupled with what I enjoyed. Basically, I fired myself as a VA, and business number three was born!

Stepping away from the oversaturated virtual assistant market was an easy choice, and stepping into B2B Digital Assistance was the obvious next move.

Earlier, I mentioned it wasn't necessarily a pretty journey. I was pregnant with my twins in early 2010. Fast-forward to August of that same year, our daughter was twenty months old. I mentioned we moved to be closer to family. My sister, her husband, their two girls, as well as my mom, lived in the area. Friday night dinners with the whole family were a regular occurrence. It's something I miss dearly to this day. One particular Friday turned my world upside down. I remember it like it was yesterday. My nieces had already started school and were working on homework or occupying their cousin in the other room. Sitting at the table was my mom, my husband, my sister, my brother-in-law, and myself. Eight months pregnant with twins, I was probably on my second helping of dinner when my world stopped. My mom told me her cancer came back, and it was terminal. She had breast cancer seventeen years prior. Everybody at the table had known for a couple of months. My mom wanted to keep it from me to protect me and my babies. She didn't want me going into early labor due to stress.

How amazing! I thought. *How selfless. How strong.*

My mom went on to live and fight cancer for two years and seven months. As a matter of fact, the day our twins were born, she had a procedure. A biopsy, I believe. She wouldn't miss the birth of those two babies. After her procedure, my sister drove her to the hospital to be with me. The nurses and staff took good care of her that day, bringing her warm blankies while we waited. All five of her grandchildren gave her the will and strength to fight so she could be there with them as long as possible.

Here I was, running my business, raising three kids under the age of two. Before this diagnosis, my mom and I planned out how and when she would be coming over. You see, she was going to be my right-hand person to help with the babies. Everything changed that night. Now, I'm a mom, a business owner, and one of the primary caretakers. (Thank you to my sister, Molly, another strong independent woman in my life who helped me out tremendously.) Luckily, my mom had a great network of friends who were also part of the caretaker committee. Running my own business was and is a blessing. I'm grateful. It gave me the freedom to be there for my mom as much as I possibly could. There were times I would drive my mom to one of her numerous appointments and nurse my babies in the parking lot.

A few short years after my mom passed, and not long after we purchased our home, my husband was laid off. Unfortunately, this morphed into about four years of inconsistent income. He'd get a job, we'd be okay, and just as we were getting back on our feet, the job or the contract would end. During this time, he was presented with his entrepreneurial journey. Here's the thing: someone needs to have consistent income. At that time, my business wasn't nearly where it is now. He did all sorts of things to support our family and our entrepreneurial goals and dreams to sustain us. He drove for Lyft and Uber for a time and worked handyman jobs. There were many times he'd be gone most of the night. Times he'd be driving or doing jobs right up until the moment he had to walk into our kids' sporting events, family dinners, etc., only to leave right after and get back at it. He did these things for me, for our family, and for the entrepreneur that lives in both of us.

The next three or four years were . . . let's just say it was a bumpy road for us financially; it was a major stress on our marriage. The year of our thirteenth wedding anniversary was especially difficult. We didn't know if we were going to make it to year fourteen. We did! We weren't struggling as much financially, but the hurt, distance, and stress of the prior couple of years were weighing heavily on us.

You know what, we made it through—together. We made it through with family, friends, and faith. It wasn't easy, and it wasn't pretty. Being an entrepreneur can oftentimes be the same way. Dan and I have a funny (well, funny to us) way of keeping things real. When our kids were born, we came up with this inside joke. Maybe it was because we're both from divorced families. We all know divorce rates are through the roof. If you didn't know, when you have twins, the divorce rate doubles! Back to our inside joke. Our agreement is, was, and always will be: if you leave this marriage, you will leave with three very heavy suitcases. Meaning, should you choose to leave, you won't just leave to go live a fabulous single life and live in a bachelor or bachelorette pad. You'll leave with three kids in tow.

Fights over money. A lot of crying, begging, pleading for him to go make some consistent income. Looking back, I was hiding. I used the excuse of him not bringing in a consistent income as my shield to deflect. I wasn't doing the things I needed to do to grow my business.

The idea of giving up on my business and going to get a J-O-B was a real discussion. We both knew I was right on the cusp of something. Call it making it, call it a success, call it a breakthrough, call it whatever you want. Giving up on something ten years in, and three businesses later, is a hard pill to swallow. We came into some money, not a lot of money, but breathing-room money. An opportunity presented itself to work with a coach. We didn't *have* the money to hire this person. We chose to make it a priority, and that's exactly what we did. Why did I need a coach? Because ten years into this entrepreneurial journey, I was dealing with the same thing so many of my clients are suffering from when we first start working together:

- Sleepless nights — Check
- My kids begging me to work less — Check
- Relationship struggling — Check
- Considering getting a regular job — Check
- People wondering why I was still doing this — Check
- Imposter syndrome — Check

I found myself stuck—stuck in the place of wanting to grow my business, but not identifying as a salesperson. Even talking about sales made me feel icky. So we're super-duper clear, without sales, you do not have a business. I have a deep, deep understanding of those items above. Good news, I solved my problem and now I get to do the same thing for my clients. Sell (or if you're like me, grow your business) without *feeling* like you're selling. I didn't even like to talk about sales back in the day. I've learned to get comfortable talking about sales activities. It all comes down to activity. Now I work with amazing women in the online space. Mostly coaches, consultants, and service providers who know they are amazing at what they do. They just can't seem to get out of their own way. Be it their messaging, how they show up online, their programs, their inaction, or not knowing the next step to take. Specifically, it comes down to the strategies people learn from me on when and how to automate or delegate certain parts of their business. Clients come to me for the vision and attention I'm able to put on their business.

Hopefully, we can all agree peanut butter and jelly is a pretty good combination, right? I like to think of myself as the PB&J of business. Marketing and sales is like a good PB&J—they go well together, and one without the other doesn't get the same results! Every day I get the pleasure of working with amazing women. I have the privilege of watching them grow and scale their businesses.

This was my journey. Not all paths to entrepreneurship are this trying, but some will be. Yours may be an easy path, or maybe you've already made it, whatever that means to you. I know this for sure: you have *hidden strength within.* I've not only survived the circumstances above, but I've also thrived. My business is thriving, I have a team, and we're still growing. Exciting opportunities are being presented to me on a weekly basis. I'm saying "yes" to every. Single. One. My husband and I are in a good place. While I'm writing this chapter, we're preparing to move across the country. This business gives me more freedom and choices than I ever imagined.

Now, not only do I see myself as a business owner; I am a thriving business owner/entrepreneur who is growing and scaling. I get the privilege to support and guide women who are looking for the same freedom and choices I now have. When the teacher in my kid's third-grade class asked, "Does anyone know what an entrepreneur is?" my daughter's arm practically shot up like a rocket as she answered, "Yes, my mom is an entrepreneur!" and proceeded to explain what that meant.

What is your *why* or purpose for your business?

If you were to ask me years ago, my *why* would've been to make some money so I could stay at home with the kids. I did just that. I made some money and I was able to stay at home with our kids. When all three of our kids went off to school, I decided it was time to get serious about my business. That's what I did.

Remember those years of struggle I mentioned? Part of the problem was not being super clear on who I served. Men, women, online businesses, brick-and-mortar businesses—industries all over the map. Ugh, it was exhausting!

The turning point for me was a recurring theme in my life. Women! At the time, I was working with a couple of pretty amazing women who served primarily women. I attended a local women's empowerment event, and I invited a couple of business owner girlfriends. One of them posted a picture on her social, which had a ton of engagement. Then, she said something like, "We should do this in our area." That's all it took for the four of us (The Fearless Foursome) to create our side hustle. We created our own local women's empowerment and networking group. Next, there was an opportunity to join a program with some of my peers. This program was going to be focused on women. Do you see the theme here? Women! The universe was not just calling me to serve women. It was like, *I'm going to put women at the forefront of everything you do.*

There is something special that happens when women come together. You're reading this book because women *have* come together. When we can cut the drama, see our worth, believe that we can do whatever the heck we want, drop the *shoulds, coulds,* and *woulds,* we are freakin' unstoppable!

Cue Beyoncé's "Run the World (Girls)." Please pause here and go listen to that song—very, very loudly. Then, take a minute and acknowledge how amazing you are. I just did!

Today, my *why* is rooted in my strength as an independent woman. I was raised by a strong independent woman and I take pride in this attribute. Not to mention, the strong independent women I have the privilege of serving and collaborating with.

If you've never done the 7 Levels Deep exercise, please add it to your to-do list, it will help you discover your *why* to self-motivate, accomplish goals, and live a purposeful life. You may need to or want to do it more than once. In my experience, when you do this exercise, different things come up. While my seven levels may change each time I do the exercise, I end up with the same result.

What is one of your greatest failures that ultimately led to success?

One of my greatest failures was and is imposter syndrome. I say "was" and "is" because it's something I will never stop working on. So many of us struggle with imposter syndrome. Especially women. If we think about it, it makes sense. We've always compared ourselves to other women. Why would business owners be any different? Thank goodness we are moving toward inclusion, mindset work, and more collaboration as a society.

When imposter syndrome pops up for me, I push myself to do the things that combat it. It's always the things that might be a little uncomfortable at first, and it usually includes getting visible. Here's the cool part: as soon as you do the activities to combat it, things start changing. It can start changing as quickly as you can snap your fingers.

Another one of my mindset tricks is a visual reminder. When you have a moment, google the 2 percent mindset. There's a great image showing all the things we do inside our comfort zone (aka the 98 percent). Then, there are all the things that happen when we choose to live outside our comfort zone (aka the 2 percent mindset). This image is printed out and hung on the wall next to my desk. I am constantly reminding myself to live and be present in the 2 percent.

This has allowed me to show up even when I'm scared. To launch new programs, workshops, training, and high-end coaching programs. Do it when you're scared. I recall the first time I said, "That'll be five thousand dollars to work with me for three months." Scared, I sat quietly as I waited on my client's reply. Long ago, someone told me, "The person who speaks first during a sales conversation loses." The client said yes with no hesitation! You know what, I hadn't even fully built out the program yet. I had the framework, the bullet points, and that's it. Do me a favor: do not let imposter syndrome hold you back for one minute longer. There are people in this world who need you. Consider it a disservice not to invite those people into your world.

If you lost everything today, what would you do for the next thirty days to generate income?

First and foremost, I would focus on the relationships I've built. If I had an immediate need for cash, I'd do something that provided quick cash, like a waitressing job. My next plan would be to start another business. It's such a great time to start a business. You can be up and running today or tomorrow!

I would watch what was happening on online platforms like social media and Upwork. These are powerful tools right at our fingertips. People tell you exactly what they need. Find the challenge that prevents people from achieving their goal and solve it. That's what I do now. It's very easy to listen, have good conversations with people (hello, sell without *feeling* like you're selling), and come up with a solution to solve their problem. Talk to people.

Here's something I've learned about myself over the years: I'm great once I get a warm lead on the phone. Something I see many entrepreneurs (including myself back in the day) struggle with is their ability to be flexible. They've built out their programs or services, but the warm lead wants X and the entrepreneur is unable or unwilling to give them X. Maybe X is the wrong price, the wrong time commitment, etc. Try this: get on the phone to determine if you're able to solve their problem. Their problem might not fit nicely in your program or package, but that's okay. If we show up and serve them well, they will eventually end up in one of our nicely packaged programs or service anyway.

How can people connect with you?

I can be found at PattyMRogers.com and on LinkedIn @PattyMRogers.

THE SECRET TO BLENDING YOUR PERSONAL AND PROFESSIONAL LIFE IS THE ONE THAT MATTERS. STOP TRYING TO BE EVERYTHING TO EVERYONE ALL THE TIME.

Micaela Royer

CHAPTER 20

MAKE IT HAPPEN BY MICAELA ROYER

"I need you to figure this out."

Those are the seven words that came out of my boss's mouth that changed my life forever as he sat across the table from me at our weekly meeting spot.

I was twenty-one and felt like I was sitting in the ruins of a dying dream. I had left college at nineteen to test the waters as a professional dancer in Los Angeles. Like many other dancers, I had big dreams of becoming the next backup dancer for Katy Perry and finding myself in commercials for big brands like Target and Pepsi.

My dance career in LA wasn't all glamour and glory. It was full of several part-time jobs, scraping money for rent, and sitting in traffic all day just to take a sixty-minute dance class where I *might* get noticed and have my big break.

When I landed my first full-time job without a college degree, I immediately dove into the comfort of security and stopped chasing dance gigs. This felt like a huge step up for me.

During our weekly meeting, my boss slid his computer over to me with a software login to write down. My job was simple: figure it out! He wanted me to learn how to make the business more money with marketing automation. From there, I became *obsessed* with learning the software. I signed up for every training possible with the company and eventually started experimenting by building systems to help me with my other jobs.

After years of trial and error, I cracked the code to streamlining my desk job at the dance studio. My contact at the software company started asking me how I would sell apps, and then I realized I had become a certified partner and could actually make money setting it up for other dance studios! I knew that I would have my own business one day, but I did not expect that it would be in technology.

Now I own The Streamlined Studio, a virtual marketing agency that works with dance studios worldwide. We help dance studio owners enroll more students and work less with the power of marketing automation. Our team works with each client to design the perfect enrollment process for their studio using automated emails, texts, task reminders, and more.

What is your *why* or purpose for your business?

I struggled so hard to keep up with my daily tasks as a dance teacher, studio admin, and social media manager. Once I cracked the code to streamlining dance studio growth with automation and started seeing results, I knew I was called to share this solution. When I streamlined our systems with automation, I had more time to focus on my students and started to enjoy my job again. And now that I've seen studio owners gain time back to spend with their family, increase their revenue, and finally feel happy again with their business, this is what I live for! I want every dance studio owner to fall asleep at night knowing their leads are being followed up with, their clients feel connected, and they are on the path for growth.

I crave that light-bulb moment with a studio owner when they finally see all the working pieces come together. The icing on top of the cake is when I see a studio owner actually enjoying their free time on social media.

What are the biggest mistakes you see new entrepreneurs making?

Here are the top three I've seen in my career:

Biggest Mistake #1—Overthinking

When I was chasing my dance career, I waited way too long to commit. I would make excuses about traffic or money when in reality, I was just scared of not being "ready." When I look back on it now, I realize this was a defense mechanism to keep me from being told that I wasn't good enough. Ouch.

If I would have just jumped sooner, went to more classes, and ditched my story of "not being ready," I probably would have been signed by an agency and booked more gigs. That's the first time I've ever said this out loud, so I hope you read it five more times, write it down, and just freaking go for it. I wish that I would have. Stop hesitating because you're afraid. You'll figure it out along the way, and that's okay. It will be messy, and you won't feel ready. But you will *never* feel ready.

Biggest Mistake #2—Jack-of-all-trade-itis

It's a disease that affects thousands of entrepreneurs: jack-of-all-trades-itis means you feel like you have to do everything yourself. You hoard all the work because no one else can do it as well as you, or you're afraid to pay an expert. You might also say that you're a control freak and you have no one to delegate to. You carry an invisible load that no one can see and you're resentful because of it. You wish that you could make a bigger impact, but you're stuck spinning your wheels doing all the things.

This was me at the dance studio, and I *never* wanted to give anything up, but I later realized that was just my ego getting in the way. I learned that you have to drop your ego at the door and ask for help when you want to truly make an impact. Make lists of what you're doing that doesn't light you up, and start delegating. It's amazing how much more you can create when you have the room in your mind to think.

Biggest Mistake #3—Always need to be the smartest person in the room

I see a lot of entrepreneurs working without a business or personal development coach because they don't think they need one. You might even feel intimidated and jealous when you're not the smartest person in the room. If you're feeling either of these things, I encourage you to check your dang ego and challenge yourself to join conversations with folks who are ahead of where you are. I thought I couldn't afford a coach and I regret telling myself that story.

When I look back on the times with the most growth in my life, I realize I had a close mentor. My first coach was a life coach in the back room of a dancewear store. She taught me how to dream, manifest, and jump. That's when I made the decision to move back to Indiana to be with my family and give 100 percent to building The Streamlined Studio.

I was looking for a business coach after that, but instead a personal development and high-performance coach came into my life. We spoke on the phone once a week and worked through all of my junk. I realized how I was projecting my own insecurities of starting a company onto my friends and family. I was playing small out of fear of being judged. Finally, I got my own office space to clear my head and finally stopped treating my business like a hobby.

When I finally got out of my own way and stopped using my personal life as an excuse to grow my business, I started working with a business coach. It was the perfect timing for this because I had done so much inner work that my daily life didn't feel like a distraction. I knew what I wanted. I wanted to build a company that would serve dance studios all around the world, a company that gives me the freedom to live wherever, raise a family, and make a huge impact. A few months after working with my business coach, everything felt like it was starting to fall into place except for one thing. I couldn't get pregnant. Everyone else around me could, though! And that's when I hired a second business coach. I know it doesn't make much sense when I say that, but let me explain. A deep part of me knew that each time I worked with a coach, I was preparing for that next level of blessing and responsibility. When I looked at my life, I knew I wasn't prepared to run my company and raise a baby at the same time, which made me realize that maybe I wasn't getting pregnant because I wasn't ready for the responsibilities that came with that blessing. Believe it or not, after a few months of prepping my business, I finally saw those two pink lines. As I'm writing this, I'm about halfway through my pregnancy. I've eaten my body weight in sunflower seeds and cried enough tears to fill Lake Michigan.

Everything is still not "in place" for me, and I realize that it will always evolve. I hope that by reading this, you realize if you want to level up and manifest your freaking dreams, you have to do these three things: stop hesitating, learn to delegate, and put a coach in your corner. Every time I felt like I was in a rut, it was because I wasn't doing those three things and it was working against me. Entrepreneurship is already hard enough. Don't make it harder.

Which activities do you perform that generate the majority of your revenue?

Easy: delegate and sell. I used to think that if I did the work to fulfill my clients' projects, I would make the most money. I was wrong! My biggest asset to the company is building relationships with future clients, creating marketing campaigns, and sharing our solutions. I can train folks to do the technical work, but I can't give them my spirit to spread to the world.

How have you diversified your revenue streams within your business?

This question challenged me because I was certain that I needed to simply list out my services and products that produce our revenue streams, but I think what you need to hear is how I came up with my product and service menu.

If you don't have a product or service created, that's your first step. Determine the people you want to help and then make a list of the challenges they face. Once you have that list, make a list of your superpowers. When you see where these two lists meet, you have identified your purpose and your first stream of revenue. Congratulations! You've just completed a task that many folks take years to accomplish.

For me, I started with setting up marketing automation to help dance studio owners streamline their enrollment process. They were struggling with spreadsheets and manual tasks, and I'm good at simplifying and automating. Do you see how it works?

Now let's look at how you can diversify your revenue streams to serve that same group of people. What other problems or challenges are they facing that you can solve with your top superpowers?

In my personal example, I found another challenge that dance studio owners face is with social media. If they have it, they aren't posting consistently or with a clear strategy. Many of them are struggling to see results because they don't know how to create a clear strategy or they are just too busy putting out fires. I've noticed throughout my career that I'm excited about creating this plan for studio owners and I'm good at creating organic social media content. My second stream of revenue is our social media membership where we create social media content templates for our members. Now they can post consistently without creating a single thing from scratch, which saves them a ton of time! Are you catching on?

Finally, think of one more thing. What else makes you excited and how can you help this same group of people? You might be questioning why I'm not telling you to dip into helping other groups of people, and there is a very good reason for that. You see, if you go out of your way to create something for another group of people (another niche), you are introducing your brand to a whole new audience you need to spend time, money, and energy to capture, nurture, and convert. That doesn't sound like a good use of your time, does it?

If there's something that you're passionate about, but it's not something you can offer with the time and resources you have, here's what you need to do: Find someone who can and partner with them. We have always wanted to offer paid social media advertisements, but it's not something my team can take on, so we've partnered with another agency to provide this service to our clients. This is now a fourth stream of revenue for us.

My secret: build your niche with your superpowers and be your authentic self.

What hard lessons have you learned that could have been avoided?

Being liked doesn't make you successful. Success comes from setting boundaries and saying no.

I used to bend over backward for everyone around me because I thought that being liked would make me more successful, and all it really did was leave me feeling exhausted and empty.

I would downplay my work to help out a friend who really could have waited until I was finished. I would skip my morning routine to hop on a call with a client I could have scheduled for later. I came last in every single scenario because I felt guilty about putting myself first. I really needed to learn how to say no to plans, projects, phone calls, etc. that didn't align with my goals or bring me joy.

The main goal of setting boundaries is to protect yourself so you can be the best possible version of yourself. Just because someone asks you to do something doesn't mean they will hate you if you say no. I will still drop almost anything for my family, but I am a lot pickier about how I spend my time because that's something I will never get back. When you start setting boundaries, it might feel terrible. You might even feel guilty about doing it because you've trained the world around you to control your schedule, and now you're taking charge. Once you start seeing the fruits of your boundary setting, it will get easier. Here are a few ways for you to start setting boundaries:

- Put important projects, events, and deadlines on your calendar and say no to everything else that tries to steal that time.
- Set aside untouchable time each day and determine the rules. This could be with yourself, your dogs, your family, your friends, or your spouse. During this time, you do what you want to do and only you can determine the rules that can break that. My untouchable time is in the morning with my morning routine, but if my husband or family needed me to take them to the emergency room, I would quickly drop what I was doing. If a client called before the office opened, I wouldn't.
- What does your product or service include and what does it not include? You may not be able to think of everything up front but try your best to draw a line in the sand where you will go the extra mile and where you won't. How many hours of calls or labor will you give? What kind of work will you do at this rate? What are extra things they may want that are not included in the scope of this agreement? This is critical for when you have a team. If you don't set this boundary at the beginning of the business relationship, you will work yourself to the ground and kiss profit goodbye.

Don't be afraid to charge for the extra things! If you're giving more value, you deserve to be compensated for it.

- What is okay and not okay to do with your work? Can someone take what you gave them and share it with a friend? I didn't set this boundary in the beginning because I thought the world was an honest place. For the most part, it is, but there are a few bad apples that will try to shortcut your prices and steal your work. P.S. If you're looking at getting a trademark or copyrighting your work, find a trustworthy lawyer and do it right.

What have you found helps with blending your personal and professional life?

I love how this doesn't say *balance*. So many people ask how to *balance* your life, and that's just not how it works.

The secret to blending your personal and professional life is the one that matters. Stop trying to be everything to everyone all the time.

I took the week off work to focus on writing this chapter, and there are several things that I had to say no to, like meetings with my team, consultations, and projects. But as I'm sitting here, I realized that I said yes to so much more this week, like drinking coffee in my backyard, watching my three dogs run around and play, and finally sharing some of my deepest thoughts with you. It's a beautiful thing to stop and take in where you're at in life, and I think that with the popular hustle mentality, it's so easy to forget that.

Do yourself a favor: break up with the world balance and be okay with that. The worst feeling in the world is guilt. Guilt that you're not spending enough time with your family or your customers or yourself. Give yourself grace. Balance and blending will look different in every season of your life, and that's okay.

What self-care, routines, and habits do you have to maintain good health?

Before my fingers hit the keyboard every day, I make sure to spend time with myself. I don't check my emails, social media, messages, etc. I open YouTube or Spotify to listen to a motivational podcast, a sermon, or uplifting music. While I'm listening, I'll make my coffee, eat some breakfast, and get ready for the day.

Whenever I skip my morning routine, I don't feel like I have the intention that I want for the day, and it turns into an anxiety-driven chaotic mess. I work on things that are not really moving me closer to reaching my goals, and then I get anxious about the thought of wasting a day. I know this may sound basic, but if you don't give yourself time, no one will. My morning routine is nonnegotiable.

What is the most worthwhile investment you have made for your business?

Coaching. Hands down. Without coaching, I would be a very lonely and unsuccessful entrepreneur. I wish that I wouldn't have hesitated to hire someone. Everyone needs a coach, and I hope you learned this when you read through my answer about mistakes I see most entrepreneurs making.

If you lost everything today, what would you do for the next thirty days to generate income?

What is *everything*? Is it my business, my family, my friends, my possessions, or all of it? If I'm being honest, I have no clue what I would do if I lost everything today. I have always thought that losing everything would kill me. But you want to know what's really odd? Why is losing everything so scary if I came from nothing to begin with? At least this time, I'll know what not to do! Maybe it's scary because there are more people counting on me now than before, but who better to build up from nothing than someone who's done it before?

I started my business when I was living in a garage in Los Angeles. I had a couple hundred dollars in my bank account, two dogs, a shrinking friend group, and a huge vision. If I can build a six-figure business, marry my dream guy, buy a house, and start a family from that, then there is a pretty good chance I can create success again. I would probably be so much better at it this time around anyway! So here she goes . . . This is what I did before when it felt like I had nothing, and this is what I would do today if I lost it all.

Step 1: Dream big

I would spend as much time as I could crafting what I wanted for my future. Decide what I wanted it to look and feel like. What would I be doing in this ultimate dream? What would I be wearing? What would I be eating? Who would be with me? (If you're reading this and rolling your eyes, I get it. I thought it was crazy too, but trust me, it works.)

Step 2: Work backward

Next, I would imagine my ultimate dream on the other side of the room I'm sitting in right now. If I were to tell you that I could achieve that dream at this very moment, you would *definitely* roll your eyes. This is because there is a huge gap between myself and this dream. Now we have to fill in that gap and define the stepping-stones. These are not set in stone, but they are a guide that can help me to at least start moving forward. What would my life look like right before I reached that ultimate dream? What would I be doing? Who would be with me? I would paint the entire picture and then take a step back each time until I found myself where I am today. Now I have a road map to help me move forward.

Step 3: Prune

Even if I don't have much of anything at this point, I will cut out anything that does not belong in my ultimate dream or at least my next step. When I was first designing my current life, I had a sticky note on my wall that said, "If you want to fly, you have to give up everything that weighs you down." This could mean selling possessions, removing myself from an environment, or quitting a habit like sleeping in. I would evaluate every element of my life and determine if that was a distraction, a spark of joy, or a building block. In the past, I had to remove myself from an unhealthy relationship and ditch the self-proclaimed starving artist story that I was telling myself. This is a difficult step, but it's not something you can avoid if you want to move toward your ultimate dream.

Step 4: Build

Now that I have a clean slate and a clear vision, it's time to start generating income in a way that fulfills me without the weight of my past or limiting beliefs. I would document all the knowledge I currently have and grow my email list to start sharing that information with the folks I want to help. This is starting to sound like I would begin a coaching program, and that's honestly what I thought I was going to do when I created The Streamlined Studio. I thought I was going to teach dance studio owners how to streamline and automate their enrollment process. These conversations turned into me running a done-for-you agency, and that's how I see this going as well. I would begin coaching the people I want to help and I'd learn how to fill in the gaps to help them further. What tools, resources, or services could I create and sell to support their journey? Then I would create just that.

Most folks might tell you to skip the first two steps and just start selling everything that you have to generate capital and create whatever you're good at, but if you want to make a lasting impact, you need to be intentional about every move you make. If you just start without a direction, how do you know what you need to take with you or what your first move would be? Dream, work backward, prune, and build.

If I lose everything tomorrow, I will probably be so paralyzed with feelings of shock and failure that it would be difficult to think straight. So if you see me losing everything after you've read this, and if I'm not following these steps, you have every right to call me out on my shit and I genuinely hope that you do.

How can people connect with you?

To connect with me or learn more about what we do for dance studios, visit thestreamlinedstudio.com.

I'VE SINCE COME TO REALIZE THAT I CAN'T FIX EVERY SITUATION AND THAT MY INABILITY TO MAKE THINGS WORK OUT FOR THE BEST EVERY TIME IS NOT NECESSARILY A FAILURE ON MY PART.

Cindy Zuelsdorf

CHAPTER 21

STORYTELLING THROUGH AUTOMATION BY CINDY ZUELSDORF

My life changed in a matter of minutes. Things had just gone bad, really bad, and I couldn't bring myself to walk back into the place I called *work*. When I walked out the door, I went from years of having a steady paycheck to no income—and no idea what to do next.

When I started with that company, there were two employees: me and the owner. Over time, that number grew to about fifty. I spent many years there, first selling equipment to TV stations like ABC, Sky, and NASA TV. I'd put equipment in a suitcase, get on a plane, and fly to another state or another country and sell solutions to broadcast engineers. Eventually, I headed up all the sales and marketing and service, and I loved a lot of it. I worked to make it a very empowering place—and one that would give the people in my marketing group a way to be their best selves, to be awesome.

Slowly, though, I realized some really bad stuff was going on around me. I hadn't been completely oblivious, but it got worse and worse until the dysfunction was untenable. While working to make a great environment for my team, I saw people around me being treated terribly. And me too. One day the breaking point came, and I left.

I had no plan. After I resigned, I cried for what seemed like months. Every day, I asked myself what I should do. It was hard, but I just focused on taking one step forward day by day. I'd wake up, sit on the couch, ask the universe what to do that day, do my very best to bring positive thoughts into my head, and make every effort to take one step forward. Okay, some days were one step forward, two steps back, but somehow I endured and moved forward.

Wonderful people I'd met or worked with in the past were calling me all the time, saying things like, "Hey, when you figure out what you're going to do, let me know." But my world changed when Caryn asked me, "What did you love at your last job?" I started listing off what I loved, and she stopped me when I came to marketing automation. "Tell me about that," she said, and so I did.

I hadn't known that marketing automation would resonate so much for me, but it did, and one thing led to another. I made a decision to start up a business built on marketing automation. I knew I could potentially do it independently, but I took a chance to see if some industry colleagues would partner with me. It seemed like a good idea, so I went for it; ultimately, I wound up running my own marketing automation business, Kokoro Marketing.

What is your *why* or purpose for your business?

My *why* for starting my business was pretty clear: I had to pay the bills. But why did I choose to start a company myself instead of going to work somewhere else? I had worked in high tech and start-up for a while, so I knew that I'd be working a zillion hours a week if I went to another company. I didn't want that. I'm not afraid of hard work and long hours, but I also wanted to spend time with my daughter, volunteer at her school, and be with my husband and family.

That was my initial *why*. But then later, having my agency and doing marketing automation, I realized that what lights me up is helping my clients tell their stories more efficiently so they can spend their time working with customers, inventing new things, or just doing what they love and do best. Then I could use marketing and marketing automation as a storytelling tool that helps them get the word out to sell their cool product or service. And that is part of why I like doing it.

About three years into the business, I paused and asked myself, "What are the things that work the best for my clients?" I sat down with some sticky notes, jotting down each campaign or marketing tactic on its own note, and tried to figure it out. After creating piles of notes and sorting through them, I came up with seven things that work the best. I went on to create a book and a course: *7 Marketing Basics*. Now I help people apply those basics to their marketing, whether they're just starting out in business or responsible for the marketing at a company.

It's funny because I always considered myself a rebel, willing to reinvent the wheel, and now I realize, "Oh, having systems is actually good!"

Which activities do you perform that generate the majority of your revenue?

My primary offers are digital courses, ongoing monthly marketing and marketing automation services, coaching, and done-with-you marketing. Most of my revenue comes from ongoing monthly marketing services; some clients work with us for months, while others have been with us for years. They have become friends! I also love having my courses and books for people who are more do-it-yourselfers or just want to have something super affordable. It's good to have several income streams and several ways to help and serve people, depending on what they need most.

Most marketing people feel overworked and overwhelmed and are spinning their wheels to figure out what's working in digital marketing. Most CEOs and business owners dislike doing marketing. They feel like they need to do it, but it takes time away from where they really want to spend their time. My offerings are created to solve those challenges:

- Course: My *7 Marketing Basics* digital course is for overwhelmed marketers, for people who want to get up to speed on what's working, and for entrepreneurs who need to grow their business. The course is a culmination of my doing 15,000+ hours of sales, marketing, and marketing automation, learning what works for our clients, and sharing exactly how to do it. Includes step-by-step videos, templates, and guides.
- Services: I've helped hundreds of people create marketing that works and increases business by using our ongoing monthly marketing services and marketing automation. Some favorite tools include checklists, guides, webinars, automated (smart!) email marketing, social media, video, SMS, and more. Because I worked in high tech and broadcast media previously, a fair number of our clients is in those spaces too, although not all of them. My agency, Kokoro Marketing, combines marketing automation with the clients' sales conversations and turns it into marketing that delivers results.
- Facebook: My 7 Marketing Basics Facebook group is a great place for someone to get excellent, actionable, free info they can put to use in their business instantly. I use video in the group, and that helps people to know, like, and trust me. If they want to do my courses, buy my books, or learn about working with me, they can do that too. I love giving and helping others, and this group gives me a place to share.

What hard lessons have you learned that could have been avoided?

I've come to realize that one reason I remained in a dysfunctional work environment for far too long was that I could be overly loyal.

Back then, I was scared to make a move because many things were good. I just kept turning away from the bad things, even though they were mounting and growing more terrible. I've since come to realize that I can't fix every situation and that my inability to make things work out for the best every time is not necessarily a failure on my part.

It's a hard lesson learned over many years, really, and I feel like I'm still learning that lesson today. Through this process, I've learned to trust myself more. Once I've recognized that something isn't good, I let go of it and give myself the chance to see what's coming next. I felt forced to do that when I left my job those years ago. While I had to take things day by day for a while, I did wind up finding a far better path for myself.

Now I try to apply that lesson in my business. If a team member is just not working out well, I'm quick to say goodbye. I have given myself permission to do what I need to do to feel like I treated that person fairly. Why go through two years of dissatisfaction, probably on both sides, only to come to the same end? I try to be realistic about when to say goodbye.

The same goes for working with clients. I don't like the "firing the client" phrase, but I have called clients on a few occasions to say it doesn't feel like a fit, that we should wrap things up. One time I returned all the money they had paid me. It just seemed like the best resolution. Another time, the client screamed at me, and that one interaction ultimately reinforced my decision.

I've learned to stop trying to make things work with clients when it's not a good fit. Now that I've built up a strong team, I'm even more committed to this idea. My team is more important to me than any client, and I'm not willing to let a team member put up with those kinds of challenges.

Another lesson I've learned the hard way is not to hire people who are too expensive. I've found that the costly professional who has a million certifications and charges a mega hourly fee sometimes needs more hand-holding and direction than the committed go-getter.

A related lesson for me is this: stop trying to be a superwoman! Oh, I've tried. But I think I've finally learned I can't do it all myself, or I burn out. I remember hiding in the bathroom one night to finish a project for a client. No more!

I started out working by myself, but now I rely heavily on my coworkers for our clients' day-to-day services. Having a great team that loves their work and is happy with their compensation is the best.

I started my team by getting one person to work closely with me for just a couple of hours a week. And then as the company grew, that first person took on more tasks and a couple more people joined. It wasn't obvious to me right away how to split up the work. That evolved. I know people say to draw out your whole company organization chart for the future, decide all the positions while you're small and starting, but that felt contrived for me. Instead, I iterated as I went.

Once I had my first team member, I concentrated on passing as many things to them as possible. Yes, sometimes it took longer to teach the task or just define it than it would have for me to do it myself, but I stuck to it. I kept defining and teaching tasks and growing my team.

I discovered that passing repetitive tasks to team members and keeping the outliers to myself worked best. When odd tasks came up early on, I'd try to pass them to a team member, but I found it more efficient to do them myself. I eventually started to focus on assigning repeatable tasks or those that would become repeatable or predictable at some point. Then we worked on a process or checklist for that task. I didn't worry about making the process perfect. I embrace iteration.

I also learned to stop worrying about having my colleagues work directly with clients. I used to be afraid that my clients wouldn't be satisfied working with my team, that I had to be present at all times. I felt nervous and worried that if the client knew I wasn't personally doing all the work, they'd freak out. I had to get past that in my mind! And I did.

I've successfully transitioned into having my team members work with clients. Just last week, someone was asking me how to make that change in their business. I started by cc'ing my team on client emails. Next, I began including team members in client meetings. When a new client starts to work with us, we have a kickoff meeting and introduce the team members to the client and discuss everyone's roles.

Also, I made sure everybody on the team had a company email address, even if they worked just a few hours per week, because I didn't want us to look all hodgepodge.

Another crucial lesson I learned is not to expect everyone to magically be on the same page with me—I need to communicate values and expectations to my team. At our weekly team meeting, we take turns reading our company purpose and values. Then we check in with each other on successes and things that could have gone better and share what we're working on in the upcoming week. Our daily stand-up meeting is ten or so minutes long, and everyone on the team shares what they're working on for the day and calls out any roadblocks they have. Additionally, I meet with each team member monthly to build care and trust, review what they are focused on, and talk about goals.

What is your biggest day-to-day struggle in running your business?

My biggest struggle day-to-day is keeping too much stuff in my head and neglecting to get those tasks into the team's project management tool. I feel like I'm forever improving on breaking down ideas and projects into smaller steps and pieces so I can hand them off to other team members and share the work.

I often have an idea or vision in my head about a project's result, and I can usually find a way to achieve it, but I know it's not fair to expect that of someone else. So I focus on not making assumptions but on communicating clearly. So I need to break down what the things are to get to that result.

What have you found helps with blending your personal and professional life?

Personal life and professional life feel like they are all one for me. For a minute, I tried to keep business on LinkedIn and personal on Facebook, but then I realized I'm on the planet to connect with others and decided it's all one.

I do have limits, though. I didn't have my computer on this past weekend. I did other fun things! So, it's not that I don't have boundaries around work, but I don't feel like I'm two different people. Personal life and professional life are blended for me, and I'm always seeking the perfect balance.

What is the most worthwhile investment you have made for your business?

By the time I decided to start my own business, I didn't have a ton of money put away. Because I hadn't been working for months, and I'd been crying and trying to figure out my future, I had burned through savings. But I managed to pay the course fees for the Keap marketing automation certified partner course and get myself a flight and hotel room for the duration of the training.

I'd only used Keap (Infusionsoft) marketing automation software a scant few times, and this training and certification were designed for expert users. I remember being up at night in my hotel room, thinking I would fail the final exam. I figured out a process for learning as quickly as I could and for reviewing material effectively. I befriended other trainees, some of whom are still my friends today, and learned from their insights. They were there with years of experience, and I'm asking myself, "What was I thinking?" Even though so many people kindly answered all my questions, I felt like a total black sheep. But I took the risk, and I did it! I sat for that six-hour exam, and my test score was great.

The decision to invest in the software and get me through that certification was possibly the best investment I could have made. I knew that the software could help small companies do much better with their marketing, and that's precisely what has happened. I can't count the number of companies I've helped with marketing automation.

I remember being at a later sales and marketing training and hearing, "Pick a niche, and do it." It turns out that's exactly what I have done. Being part of a community with like-minded entrepreneurs has been crucial for me. The Keap community provides a lot of sales training. There are other people to talk with and share inspiration with. Whether you participate in a group or meet with one person regularly, it's a fabulous way to keep moving forward in your business.

Sometimes, when I talk with other business owners and entrepreneurs, they say they feel so alone that they don't have anybody to talk to and bounce ideas off. My suggestion is to find another business owner to meet with once a week, a serious person, not someone who's going to cancel all the time. I meet with Sharon every Thursday and with Bill every Friday. We share wins from the week before and what we want to do for the coming week and help each other out when we feel stuck or flat. I've found this massively helpful. If you can find someone, even if they're not in your same industry, and commit to meeting with them each week, you'll benefit for sure!

If you lost everything today, what would you do for the next thirty days to generate income?

I already did that! I went from having a job and income to no income in the blink of an eye.

Today, I can honestly say that I'm so grateful it happened, even though it was the worst at the time. The worst. Here's what I did, and I'd do it again:

- Talked with friends. I spoke with colleagues in the industry I'd been working in. I picked up the phone and called people. Got their suggestions and let them know I was open to working.
- Made new connections through friends and business associates.
- Found other businesspeople to meet with weekly. Regularly met with a business coach who was 100 percent paid for through the Small Business Association.
- I made a list of everyone I could think of and put that list into my database. Used Keap CRM and marketing automation to keep track of prospects, tasks, follow-up, promotion, and sales, all in one place.
- Looked for strategic partners to work with. Offered to teach something to a business association group, found ways to partner with someone on a product/service.
- Listened a lot to my inner voice, and asked what to do, trusted myself, no second-guessing. (Okay, just tried to limit the second-guessing as much as I could!)
- Listened to positive audiobooks at night while going to sleep.
- Decided on a way to "serve my former self." I came up with a business that served sales and marketing people because I was working in sales and marketing in my previous job and knew the needs of someone in that position.

- Invested in special training that set me apart from other sales and marketing professionals. I did the Keap–certified partner training before officially starting my business. (This proved to be very important. Later, other marketing people, who I perceived as more experienced and more senior than me, called me and asked for help finding work. I feel sure that my choice to narrow in on marketing automation made it easier for me to get clients than those who were jack-of-all-trades marketing types.)
- Figured out three products/services I could offer and went for it. Iterated as I learned more.
- Didn't let perfection get in the way of progress. I wasn't perfect, I didn't know everything, but I knew a lot and I could help anyone who asked for marketing help. So I did!
- Worked every day, didn't treat it like a hobby.
- Set goals for how much money I needed for the next few months just to get rolling. Worked to get my first two clients.
- Decided on goals (some big, some small) and did at least one thing every day to take me toward those goals. I avoided doing things that didn't take me to the goals. Even when you can't see the whole route (most of the time!), you can always take the next step toward your destination.

How can people connect with you?

I can be found at kokoroinc.com and 7MarketingBasics.com.

CONCLUSION

What we want for you to take away from this book is that there are so many different and amazing ways to build a business. You don't have to struggle, learn, and go at it alone. You don't have to fear failure or feel like you need to know all the things before you get started.

Why? Because we have your back. We've all experienced the start-up phase, leveling up, and juggling work and life. Pivoting and evolving as we learn and grow. When mistakes are made, we move forward wiser and more prepared. It's just a part of owning and growing a business. It's not always pretty or glamorous, but it is rewarding.

Collectively, female entrepreneurs are the most generous, intelligent, and empowered people on the planet. We believe in collaboration and community over competition. We believe that when one of us succeeds, we all win. We are here to cheer and celebrate every milestone and victory.

To be clear, we want *you* to have the business and lifestyle of your dreams. Whether that's a seven-figure business or a part-time side hustle. It's up to you and how you want to structure your life.

In order to create a business that supports your *why*, you need to be clear on your goals and your mission.

A goal or mission is anything you want it to be. Your business, your definition of success. It's whatever feeds your passion and fuels your soul.

Ask yourself: What is one thing I can do today to build a business I love and get paid for it?

The female entrepreneurs in this book have given you many. Start with one.

Implement it. Then try another one. Rinse and repeat. It's about building momentum toward fulfilling your *why*.

Along your journey, we encourage you to partner up with other entrepreneurs and support each other's businesses. This book is a testament to how impactful and significant those relationships can be. Every single person who participated in this project is connected in one way or another. Some of us are clients of each other's businesses, some share the same mentor or mastermind, and others are connected through friends or colleagues.

By writing this book together, we have become respected friends and future business partners. And as a reader, you now have a seat at our table. We welcome you to join the conversation and connect with us and engage.

To all our future successes!

Patricia

Lindsey

ABOUT PATRICIA WOOSTER

Patricia is a former corporate software executive turned traditionally published author of thirteen books. She is the founder of WoosterMedia that transforms leaders, entrepreneurs, athletes, influencers, and thought leaders into published authors who amplify their message through high-impact books.

She has worked on over 350+ traditional publisher projects and helped countless others self-publish their books. She coaches people through the process of creating a transformational experience for their readers by mastering their message, engaging with their readers, and adhering to the high standards set by the traditional publishing industry. Her clients have landed agents, publishing contracts, speaking opportunities, and best-seller status.

ABOUT LINDSEY ARDMORE

Lindsey started Star Tower Systems with a dream and a three-day-old baby. She realized that she could start a business doing what she loved instead of working her life away for someone else. Lindsey is an automation wizard and business strategist who focuses on creating peaceful experiences for business owners and their customers alike! She's known for her get-it-done attitude and her candid conversations about life and business. Her spirit animal is a honey badger.

THANK YOU

Thank You For Reading our Book!

We really appreciate all of your feedback, and we love hearing what you have to say.

We need your input to make the next version of this book and our future books even better.

Please leave us a helpful review on Amazon letting us know what you thought of the book.

Thank you so much!
Patricia Wooster & Lindsey Ardmore